Murder
at the
Brown Palace

MURDER
at the
BROWN PALACE

A True Story of
Seduction & Betrayal

Dick Kreck

Fulcrum Publishing
Golden, Colorado

Library of Congress Cataloging-in-Publication Data

Kreck, Dick.
  Murder at the Brown Palace : a true story of
seduction & betrayal / Dick Kreck.
  p. cm.
Includes bibliographical references and index.
  ISBN 1-55591-463-2 (pbk. : alk. paper)
  1. Murder—Colorado—Denver—Case studies. I. Title.
HV6534.D45 K74 2003
364.15'23'0978883—dc21
  2002151255

Editorial: Ellen Wheat, Don Graydon, Daniel Forrest-Bank
Cover and interior design: Alyssa Pumphrey, Brazen Husky Design
Formatting: Anne Clark
Cover images: View of the Brown Palace Hotel at Seventeenth Street
    and Broadway in downtown Denver, Colorado, circa 1910.
    Photograph by William Henry Jackson, courtesy of the Colorado
    Historical Society (CHS.J2527). Photograph of Isabel Patterson
    Springer, courtesy of the Denver Public Library, Western History
    Department.

Printed in the United States of America
0 9 8 7 6 5 4 3 2

Fulcrum Publishing
16100 Table Mountain Parkway, Suite 300
Golden, Colorado 80403
(800) 992-2908 • (303) 277-1623
www.fulcrum-books.com

For my grandkids, who just keep coming

Contents

FOREWORD

High society. Adultery. Drugs. Multiple murder. All this and more, set in Denver's grand old hotel, the Brown Palace.

Hollywood murder-mystery writers could not have contrived a thriller as chilling as this factual account of a double murder on the night of May 24, 1911. It happened in the Marble Bar of the Brown Palace Hotel while the cause of it all, Denver's most whispered-about society vamp, waited upstairs in her suite.

The talk of the town for years, the deadly dispute over the city's most beautiful woman is now a faded memory. Even in 1911, when the affair exploded in the newspapers and in country club gossip, no one pulled the whole story together or tracked down the once passionately involved principals who went their separate, lonely ways.

The two men fighting over Isabel "Sassy" Patterson Springer did not include her unsuspecting husband, John W. Springer, the wealthy owner of Cross Country Ranch, respected businessman and aspiring politician. The ambitious Springer narrowly lost one of the most crooked elections in Colorado history, the 1904 Denver mayoral race, which Robert W. Speer won with the help of ten thousand phony votes. Springer was well known and well liked by Coloradans, including his seductively beautiful wife, twenty years younger than he.

Following the Brown Palace shootout, Denver wanted vengeance, something to end a series of murderous domestic disputes that outraged the citizenry but put no one behind bars.

Frank Henwood, a pretty boy from back east, became a target for the forces of righteousness in two quirky, explosive trials.

Here, for the first time, is the complete story of Colorado's most spectacular crime of passion. Dick Kreck, an indefatigable reporter who sticks to the facts, treats readers to the full lurid tale and its impact on a youthful western city struggling to cleanse itself of sin in all forms. A fascinating study of the supposedly better morals of "the good old days," it is also a revealing look at journalism and the legal system when both were far more colorful and combative than they are today. Finally, it is a study in sexism, showing how a woman was universally condemned for doing what a man was expected to enjoy.

Kreck, who worked at the *San Francisco Examiner* and the *Los Angeles Times* before joining *The Denver Post* in 1968, knows Denver inside out. *The Post*'s senior columnist has long been the journalist that city watchers go to first.

After two years of researching *Murder at the Brown Palace*, Kreck delivers a love story, a murder mystery, and a court-room drama. This account is also a revealing history of how a brash young city's Victorian sensibilities were crushed.

Ironically, this most sensational murder case came during Denver's Progressive Reform Era, whose puritanical cleansing was aimed at sinners such as Sassy. The year after the murders, reformers ousted the easygoing Mayor Speer. They shut down Denver's Market Street red-light district in 1912. Four years later, voters imposed statewide prohibition on hard-drinking Denverites. Not only Sassy and her lovers but all Coloradans were herded into a new and puritanical age.

—Thomas J. Noel ("Dr. Colorado")

Acknowledgments

Nothing in this book is made up. Not by me, anyway. This tale of love, lust, betrayal, and murder that shook Denver society in 1911 reads like a television soap opera or a tragic opera, but it's all true. No one intimately involved escaped unscathed.

There are many people to thank for helping me shape a fuller picture of the incident at the Brown Palace Hotel, the trials and their outcomes, and for support through the days of researching, writing, and rewriting. Among them:

Peter Aeby and Deborah Dix, who gave me access to historical records at the Brown Palace; Lew Cady; Irene Frye Gay; Ellen Wheat, who "got" it from the beginning; Don Graydon, my copyeditor, whose sharp eye averted numerous blunders; the staff of the Genealogy and Western History Department of the Denver Public Library; my wife, Victoria Gits; David F. Halaas, former chief historian, Colorado Historical Society; Johanna Harden of the Douglas Public Library; Vickie Heath; Joe Hoppel, who researched Tony von Phul's life in St. Louis; Corrine Hunt; former Denver Mayor Quigg Newton; Tom Noel; Bob Rector; Shea Homes; Ann Student; and Ed Will.

And, finally, my gratitude to the reporters, most of them anonymous, who labored to cover the trials, and to the editors of the city's four fiercely competitive newspapers who printed column after column of testimony that lives on, even after official court documents have disappeared. The dialogue in these pages is based on contemporary newspaper accounts.

Chapter One

PRELUDE TO MURDER: "I WILL BE THERE"

SYLVESTER LOUIS VON PHUL was in a dark mood when he stepped off the Denver Limited from Kansas City at Denver's Union Station on May 23, 1911.

He squinted in the bright sunlight, glanced up at the sprawling station's red stone clock tower and noted the time; it was just past 1 P.M. He wasted no time hurrying through the main waiting room and out to Wynkoop Street at the foot of Seventeenth Street, where he was confronted by a three-story steel arch whose spidery lattice would have made it an attractive topper to a wedding cake. The arch was said to weigh seventy tons and at night was illuminated by two thousand electric lightbulbs. Its pillars supported an I-beam that read "Welcome" on one side and "Mizpah," a Hebrew prayer for safe travel, on the other. It was a placid salutation for a man with a score to settle.

Even a casual observer would be struck by the visitor's athletic build, over six feet tall and nearly 220 pounds. His features were coarse but not unattractive. He wore his hair combed into a pompadour and parted on the left side. He had intense, deep-set blue eyes. The imposing von Phul, age thirty-three, was well known in his hometown, St. Louis, for his abilities as a balloon pilot and daredevil adventurer and, not incidentally, as a gentleman who was a favorite with actresses and other beautiful women.

A raggedy newsboy, who looked about ten years old and wore a tweed cap cocked over one ear, thrust a copy of that morning's *Rocky Mountain News* at him. Von Phul studied the front page and a four-column headline that screamed, "Crushes Her Husband's Head With Ax in House Where His Father Was Killed." He declined to fork over two cents, choosing instead to hail a taxi for the Brown Palace Hotel across town.

Denver, early in the twentieth century, had shaken its dusty frontier town image. Office buildings and department stores, some of them ten stories high, lined Seventeenth Street, a main thoroughfare. On either side of the street, graceful wrought-iron utility poles held street lamps. Only two years before, unsightly poles, painted white and slatted with four or five cross-members, held a web of wires that powered the newly electrified city. The street was home to the exclusive Denver Club, the impressive Equitable Building, and two of the city's better hotels, the Oxford, only a block from the station, and the Albany with its baroque façade.

Von Phul's destination was the elegant Brown Palace at the upper end of Seventeenth, crowded at midday with horse-drawn delivery wagons, bicycles, streetcars, and the newly emerging automobile. As the cab drew closer to the Brown, von Phul (pronounced, ironically in light of subsequent events, *von Fool)* mulled the first words he would say to Isabel Patterson Springer, the socialite wife of one of Denver's political and business leaders.

He wanted answers. Von Phul, one-time cowboy and automobile racing driver, was not used to being crossed. Two weeks earlier, Mrs. Springer, called by those closest to her by the pet names "Sassy" and "Belle," sent him a letter, one of many she penned to him after they had renewed their acquaintance in St. Louis in January. In it, she pleaded with him to come visit her in Denver. "I shall expect you here in a week and no later. I want you here and you must come. If you do I will tell you what you will be glad to hear, something

*Sylvester L. "Tony" von Phul.
(*The Denver Times, *May 25, 1911. Courtesy of the Colorado Historical Society)*

I cannot put down here." It was signed, "Belle." About the same time, she wrote, "If I don't hear from you today, I will take the first train tomorrow morning for Kansas City," where von Phul was visiting on business.

Though it was never proved, some in Denver's society circles whispered that the relationship between Isabel Springer and von Phul, known to his friends as Tony, stretched back to their school days in St. Louis. As a young woman, Isabel was a frequent participant in gaieties that attracted the city's young set, earning her the reputation of a social butterfly. In 1907, divorced only a few weeks from traveling shoe salesman John E. Folck, Isabel married the powerful and very rich Colorado business leader and renowned horseman John Wallace Springer in a St. Louis ceremony. She was twenty-seven years old, he was forty-seven. She was, in modern terminology, a trophy wife. She was vivacious, beautiful, and, within bounds, independent for her day. Immediately after a wedding luncheon at the Hotel Jefferson in St. Louis, the couple boarded a train for Denver.

John W. Springer.
(Courtesy of
the Colorado
Historical Society)

It was not her first trip to the Queen City. The previous summer, she had stayed at the Savoy Hotel, almost directly across Broadway from the Brown Palace, and was squired around town by Springer in one of his fine horse-drawn carriages, which were the envy of the city's equestrian set. Springer, regarded as one of Denver's most eligible bachelors after the death of his wife in 1904, was clearly smitten.

After marrying Springer, Isabel often accompanied her husband on business trips to New York City, a place with the fast-paced artistic and social lifestyle she had missed since moving to Denver and apparent domesticity. Sometimes she returned to Denver with him; sometimes she did not. She also traveled to St. Louis to visit friends, and it was on one of these trips that she fell under the spell of von Phul. Despite Isabel's marriage to Springer, von Phul remained in her life.

Isabel led a busy private life. She began writing intimate letters to von Phul in January 1911. In April, to recover from a serious though never publicly explained surgery, she

*Isabel Patterson Springer.
(Courtesy of the Colorado
Historical Society)*

traveled to Hot Springs, Arkansas, where she and the aeronaut
were often-seen companions on the party circuit. When she
returned to Denver and her husband, Isabel continued to
write to von Phul, sometimes referring to him as "Tony
Boy." Her letters showered him with endearments, including "Your little sweetheart is thinking of you" and "I wish
you were here tonight to tuck me in my little bed and kiss
me goodnight."

But von Phul was not the only object of her attention outside
her marriage. In March 1911, she was introduced to Harold
Francis Henwood, a friend and business partner of her husband, in Springer's office, and the three became close
friends. Henwood called Isabel "Sassy," and she called him
"Frank," unusual familiarities for the time. Beginning May
17, Henwood and Isabel spent five days at the Springers'
twelve-thousand-acre Cross Country Ranch, fifteen miles
south of town. Henwood was often at the Springers' spread
on the rolling grass plains. Sometimes his visits included

Frank Henwood.
*(*Denver Republican,
May 26, 1911. Courtesy of the
Colorado Historical Society)

business discussions; often it was merely social. Many times, only Isabel and Frank were in attendance.

Born in Naples, Italy, of well-to-do parents who were vacationing there when he came into the world, Henwood was tall, thin, an impeccable dresser and blessed with a glib manner. His right eyebrow rose frequently in a kind of sardonic tilt over soft blue eyes. He favored tailored three-button, blue serge suits with matching vests and often casually left the top two buttons on his jacket undone. He was a man of the world, a wanderer and a promoter of business schemes, a pre-occupation that took him many places, including South America, Canada, Alaska, California, and New York City. He left in his wake a series of ill-fated business enterprises, a failed marriage that produced two daughters, and a reputation as a sophisticated fellow who harbored a hot temper that became particularly fiery when he was drinking.

The thirty-five-year-old Henwood had appeared in Denver the previous November, bent on finding investors for the American Blau Gas Company, which was planning to build a gas plant in the city. Springer, monied and a socially active club member of the Denver community, was the ideal target for Henwood's sales pitch. Springer gave the opportunistic promoter entree to Denver's business and social circles.

❖

The socially adept Mrs. Springer thrived on compliments. Newspaper society writers commented on her flamboyant dress, her social graces, her gay dinner parties at the Brown Palace, and especially her attractive physical features. One described her as "breathtakingly lovely." As the wife of one of Denver's most respected men, she wanted for nothing. But she wanted more. Not one but two suitors showered her with attention. So ardent were they that Gene Fowler in *Timber Line*, his entertaining and frequently imaginative history of *The Denver Post*, referred to von Phul and Henwood as "the sky-riding Don Juan and the Orlando of the gas tanks." Isabel apparently couldn't decide between the two. On one hand, she wrote sweet somethings to von Phul for the last time on May 20, urging him to come to her. On the other, she met with Henwood on May 12 and asked him to get back for her "some foolish little letters," more than two dozen, she had written to von Phul. The St. Louisan, she told Henwood, was threatening to blackmail her with them.

As von Phul's train steamed across Kansas toward Denver on the morning of May 23, Henwood and Isabel were meeting in the Springers' suite on the sixth floor at the Brown, an emotional encounter at which she again asked Henwood to retrieve her letters and repeated von Phul's threat to show them to her husband one by one unless she resumed their relationship. Eager to please, Henwood agreed to ask von Phul, as a gentleman, to return the letters, but there was a string attached. He told Isabel to write a note, telling von Phul that things were over between them. She refused. The persistent Henwood dictated a letter for her to write that told the St. Louisan things were all over. He typed a copy to be given to von Phul when he arrived.

❖

Ten minutes after he reached Denver, von Phul was at the check-in desk of the Brown Palace. The hotel, constructed of Colorado red granite and Arizona sandstone, was built by Henry C. Brown and two partners on a triangular piece of land bounded by Broadway, Tremont Place, and Seventeenth Street. It opened with great fanfare on August 25, 1892, with a dinner for the Triennial Enclave of the Knights Templar. The knights and their ladies dined on a sumptuous dinner that included clams, mountain trout, filet of beef, terrapin, and Nesselrode pudding, all accompanied by vintage wines.

Built in 1892, the Brown Palace remains Denver's most gracious hotel. (Dick Kreck collection)

Brown arrived in Denver in 1860 as a carpenter and saved two hundred dollars, enough to buy 160 acres on the hills east of downtown. He became a real-estate speculator and donated ten acres of his land for the state capitol. He owned a great deal of land surrounding the capitol site, known as Brown's Bluff, and knew that if he could get the capitol built near his land, homes of the rich and influential would follow. He was right.

The hotel, originally known as Brown's Palace Hotel, cost two million dollars to build and furnish. It was then, and remains today, the last word in travel elegance. The hotel's central atrium soars eight stories, topped by an elaborate stained-glass skylight. Seven hundred intricate ironwork panels decorate the interior levels. Built with a steel frame and outfitted with a sprinkler system, it was one of the first buildings in America to be fireproof. Twenty-six carved sandstone medallions depicting animals, carved by James Whitehouse, adorn the seventh-floor exterior and still catch the eye of passersby.

In its storied history it has played host to numerous luminaries, including "Buffalo Bill" Cody, John Philip Sousa, several Barrymores, Lillian Russell, Mary Pickford, and The Beatles. Presidents from Teddy Roosevelt to Bill Clinton have stayed there. Dwight Eisenhower and his wife, Mamie, a Denver native, spent many of their vacations within its walls. The international Summit of the Eight was headquartered in the plush surroundings in 1998. Almost every Denverite has a story of a birthday, anniversary, or other affair spent there, and the lobby continues to host afternoon teas for ladies in hats.

Living amidst this splendor, sharing her new life as the belle of Denver society with her millionaire husband, was Isabel Springer. Also living at the Brown was the ambitious gas peddler Henwood, who had drifted from East Coast society to a nomadic lifestyle. In the eight months since his arrival from New York City, his charm and easy conversational manner had made him a familiar figure among Denver's privileged. Possessed of a quick temper, Henwood had built a checkered history at the hotel since moving into room 717 on November 2, 1910. There was, for example, the matter of getting drunk and pummeling a bellboy for inefficiency. And there was the night that police were summoned because he insisted, by pounding on her door, that an actress starring in the musical *Chocolate Soldier* at the Auditorium Theater answer his 3 A.M. visitation. He was fined seven dollars and kicked out of the hotel briefly for the indiscretion.

Henwood was a large part of the cause of von Phul's anger. Until the roving promoter arrived in Isabel Springer's life, von Phul was her major affinity outside of her husband, who, in addition to owning thousands of acres of ranch land in Douglas County, was a founder and vice president of Continental Trust Company, an unsuccessful candidate for Denver mayor in 1904, and a superb horseman.

❖

Isabel's husband, John Wallace Springer, had arrived in Denver in 1896 and, within a year, immersed himself in the city's business and social life. He fit in easily. He was a glad-hander, and he was good-looking, despite his oversized ears. He sported a thick mustache with eyebrows to match and his thinning hair was parted in the middle in something resembling a split comb-over. A natty dresser, he preferred shirts with extremely high collars and frequently wore jeweled stickpins in his ties.

He soon found himself in a social circle that included many of the city's most prominent citizens. He was, noted one observer, "a preeminently successful and resourceful businessman" who was "affable, genial, public-spirited, patriotic and a political leader." He was a joiner. At various times, he was a member of the National Live Stock Association (of which he was a founder and president for seven years), the Colorado Cattle & Horse Growers Association, the Denver Chamber of Commerce, the University Club, the Denver Country Club, the Colorado

Frank Henwood and Tony von Puhl kept a close eye on each other at dinner in the Brown Palace's palm-bedecked dining room the night before the shooting. (Dick Kreck collection)

Republican Club, the Overland Country Club, Stockman's Club, Gentlemen's Driving and Riding Club, the Pan-Hellenic Club, and the Denver Motor Club. In addition, he belonged to the Real Estate Exchange and the Denver Bar Association and was a trustee of the University of Denver.

Although he was an enthusiastic civic booster for Denver who numbered among his close friends influential business and political leaders, he was the loser in one of the city's most corrupt elections. He was oblivious to his wife's activities outside their marriage and to the drama unfolding at the Brown Palace Hotel.

❖

When von Phul checked in to the hotel, he was assigned room 524 but was put temporarily in 404 until his room was ready. Later, he asked to be switched to 603, near the Springers' suite, 600 and 602, whose curved corner windows overlooked the corner of Seventeenth and Broadway. When he signed in, he was handed the note Henwood had dictated to Isabel. It read,

> This is just to let you know that someone knows a great deal. Therefore, under no circumstances, telephone me or try to communicate with me in any way. Everything

is finally and absolutely off and if you wish to save your-self serious trouble with someone and his friends you will forget that you ever knew me. Personally my future is of too much consequence and I'll never risk it [here she had crossed out the word *again*]. I will send someone to you to have a final talk with you, and you must be guided by what they say. I have been forbidden to see you or hear from you in the future and I have given my word, which I propose to keep, not to see you again. I have taken this means of letting you know.

It confirmed what von Phul already suspected. There was meddling afoot.

About 4:45 P.M., Henwood sent a bellboy to pull von Phul out of the hotel's barroom and into the lobby, where Henwood and von Phul met, apparently for the first time, although some later claimed that they had clashed previously over Isabel in St. Louis. Who tipped Henwood to the burly St. Louisan's arrival isn't known. Henwood introduced himself and added, without expla-nation, "I wish to have a conversation with you regarding a sub-ject you are concerned with. I am the person referred to in the letter." Von Phul quickly agreed to a 5:30 meeting in his room.

Each man was determined to keep an eye on the other. As Henwood sat in the lobby, waiting for the appointed time to arrive, he glanced at his watch and noted it read 5:20. He spied von Phul, talking with the clerk at the front desk. Suspicious, he approached von Phul.

"Well, you're ready for me, aren't you?"

"I will be there," von Phul answered, just before he exited the hotel.

Henwood quizzed the clerk behind the counter. "Where did Mr. von Phul say he was going?" "To Daniels & Fisher," said the clerk, giving Henwood, a relative newcomer, directions to the large department store at Sixteenth and Arapahoe Streets, eight blocks from the hotel.

Furious, Henwood jumped into a taxi and headed for Daniels & Fisher.

The cab pulled up to the store's Sixteenth Street entrance, Henwood stepped out and strode in. The department store was among the city's elite shopping emporiums that included the Denver Dry Goods Co., A. T. Lewis & Son, and the Golden Eagle. Daniels & Fisher was distinguished by its 330-foot tower, inspired by the Campanile of Venice. The tallest building in town, it provided a 200-mile panorama of the Rocky Mountains to the west from its observation deck. As if coming to attention for the determined Henwood's arrival, the American flag atop the tower snapped in a brisk west wind.

In minutes, he found Isabel. Her mother and frequent companion, Amelia Patterson, was seated nearby. There was no sign of von Phul.

Henwood used the moment to chastise Isabel, who must have been alarmed to see him. "Isabel, you haven't told me the truth about this. You are going to meet von Phul here, contrary to what you promised, you would let me see him first and talk to him."

Caught off-guard, Isabel responded, "No, no I'm not."

"Now, Isabel, I know better. I know he is on his way down here. You said you wouldn't see von Phul, and now you are about to meet him. That is the worst thing you can do. When you reach a point with a person that is threatening you, the time comes for a showdown. Make him know exactly that you are not going to let him go any further."

Again she denied she'd spoken to von Phul, which was unfortunate because at that moment he walked into the conversation. His first words were directed to Henwood. "Oh, eavesdropper, you here?" Gazing at Isabel, he said, "I want to talk to this young lady alone."

"You can talk to her right here, and you can't talk to her again alone in Denver or any other place," Henwood said as he took Isabel's arm. "I am here to prevent you breaking up this home. As a friend of both John and Isabel, I will deal with you for Mrs. Springer."

This was not what von Phul had in mind. Henwood's involvement was confounding an already confused affair. He became abusive. "I have a goddamned notion to spill you all over the place," he growled, apparently not caring that "the place" was the palm-bedecked shoe department of one of the town's classiest department stores.

Henwood refused to back down. "Don't start in on me. I wouldn't let you do it."

Von Phul's language became increasingly vulgar. Trying to calm Isabel and her mother, both visibly upset, Henwood suggested that he and von Phul go back to the hotel "and talk it over in a sociable way." As they walked up the aisle toward an exit, von Phul continued to rain down profanities on Henwood. "You are a damned son of a bitch of an eavesdropper! What in the hell are you butting in for, you son of a bitch?"

Astoundingly, the two men, each unwilling to let the other out of his sight lest he double back to the department store, shared a taxi to the Brown. On the brief ride, von Phul continued to upbraid Henwood, slinging vile epithets at him. A surprisingly composed Henwood, determined to avoid a physical confrontation with the larger von Phul, pointed out that everything could be worked out. The two agreed to adjourn to 404, von Phul's room before he changed it to be nearer Isabel, and discuss it.

Once in the room, things took a more hostile turn. Von Phul closed and bolted the door. Henwood, suspicious that something more than conversation was to be exchanged, put his hand on the bulkier von Phul's right hip pocket and felt a hard object.

"You have a gun in your pocket, haven't you?"

"Yes," said von Phul, his pale blue eyes fixed on his rival.

Seeking to defuse the showdown, Henwood said, "I would like you to know I do not carry a gun. I have never carried one

*Isabel Springer's hand-written version of note to Tony von Phul. (*The Denver Times, *June 27, 1911. Courtesy of the Colorado Historical Society)*

in my life. I think a man who does is a coward. I have not come here for trouble. I want to talk with you like a man."

Von Phul walked slowly across the room and sat in a chair. Henwood remained standing.

"You are an impostor, Mr. Henwood," said von Phul.

Henwood stared, choosing his words carefully. "I am the party mentioned in the message to you. I am a very close friend of John Springer. He is the one man who made my success in Denver possible."

Von Phul looked only vaguely interested.

Henwood pressed on, drawing on his salesman's gift for words. "I understand you have some foolish letters of Isabel's. I know her as John's wife, and I have known of this thing for a long time. You have been threatening to send them, one by one, to her husband unless she left him. I have been with him every day practically since I have known him. He has helped me in a thousand different ways, both socially and in a business way."

Like a knight errant, Henwood continued his quest. Now on bended knee before his rival, he said, "I understand you are making threats. John has reached the stage in life where he needs all the comfort that there is, that can be had. He is not a young man and he is devoted to Isabel, and I know that she is devoted to him. I know that she worships him. I know that she would give anything in the world to have a free mind and be able to make John happy. For God's sake, Tony, will you break up this home?"

Henwood had made a serious misstep. Von Phul was "Tony" only to his friends, and Henwood's familiarity made him angry. He slapped the smaller Henwood, whom he outweighed by forty pounds. Henwood staggered and calmly said, "Von Phul, you are the first man who ever struck me without my returning it. I cannot afford a scene at this hotel. I still want to talk to you."

"What do you want to say?" Not waiting for a reply, von Phul snatched up a wooden shoe tree lying on a nearby table and brought it down on the left side of Henwood's forehead. The two men clutched each other and fell, von Phul on his back, his hands pinned over his head by Henwood, who seized the advantage. "I still do not want a scene," he said, hoping to put an end to the scuffle.

"All right," said von Phul.

It was a brief armistice. Henwood rose, turned, and unlocked the door. When he turned back to face von Phul, he was confronted with a revolver. Frightened, Henwood nevertheless advanced toward von Phul until the weapon was touching the pit of his stomach. He challenged, "You dirty coward, you dare not pull the trigger. You are a coward, a dirty cur."

There was an interminable pause. Henwood held his ground. Von Phul thought it over. "Get out of my room, you son of a bitch! I can't get you here because they would have it on me, but I'll get you yet and I'll get you quick."

Relieved, Henwood retreated to his room on the seventh

floor. Von Phul, angry over the day's travails, rushed upstairs to the Springers' sixth-floor suite. When Isabel opened the door, he stormed in. "You have lied to me!" he told her just before he slapped her, not for the first time. The blow caused her to stagger and nearly fall to the floor.

Von Phul angrily grabbed two photographs of Henwood that stood in Isabel's sitting room. Both bore intimate notations to the people he considered his closest friends and benefactors: "My bestest to Sassy who can bring out the best side of anyone I know. Faithfully, Frank"; and, "John and Sassy. 'Don't.' With best wishes from 'I Won't' Frank." He ripped them from their frames and tore them into small pieces. "I don't think you should have these pictures of a man who is butting in."

Isabel let him believe it was Henwood who had torn up a photo of von Phul the previous week, though she had destroyed it herself, at Henwood's request. Von Phul took a piece of Isabel's delicate blue stationery and quickly scribbled a note to Henwood: "Frankie Dear—You destroyed my picture & here is part of yours." As he prepared to leave, von Phul put a small, ragged piece of one of Henwood's photographs in an envelope with the note, then jammed the rest of the pieces into his jacket pocket. He also warned Isabel that if he ever saw her with Henwood, even in the presence of her husband, he would "fix him," one of several times over two days that he threatened his rival. Five minutes later, he left.

❖

Things were beginning to unravel and a showdown was inevitable. Frantic, Isabel Springer was trying to juggle the emotions of two ardent admirers, neither of whom was about to back down. The fleeting hours of May 23 were filled with meetings—in her rooms, in hallways, in Henwood's room, in public places.

That night, all the principals in the worsening drama

came together for supper in the hotel's dining room—at separate tables.

Von Phul and his cousin, Fred Cooke, met in the hotel lobby at 6:30 P.M. The two shook hands, causing von Phul to wince in pain. His right hand was bruised and skinned, and his thumb was dislocated from the fight with Henwood.

Von Phul, Cooke, and a third man, Fred Charles, a traveling salesman and a friend of von Phul's, headed for dinner in the hotel dining room. Shortly after the three sat down, Henwood entered the room by himself and took a table not far away in the long, narrow room whose numerous palms gave it a tropical look. As befitted the hotel, tables draped in white linen sat atop oriental rugs.

"That's the party," von Phul confided to his companions.

Things had not calmed down much after the confrontation in von Phul's room. Cooke later recalled that Henwood "was facing me but Tony's back was to Henwood. Every time I made a remark, [Henwood] either laughed or sneered." His attitude so irked Cooke that he told his cousin, "Turn him over to me and I'll kick a bale of hay out of him." "Don't bother," soothed von Phul. "He isn't worth it."

After dinner, Cooke, Charles, and von Phul got up to leave. "I have to make a few calls on clients," von Phul told his companions. As a representative of a Midwest wine distributor, von Phul's calls frequently involved sharing his company's products with proprietors. As the three men left the dining room, von Phul, knowing Henwood was watching, made it a point to stop and chat with the Springers. Isabel introduced her husband to the man with whom she had been corresponding so ardently. Unaware of the conflict swirling around his beautiful wife, Springer stood and shook von Phul's hand. "An honor to meet you," he said.

Von Phul, Cooke, and Charles hadn't reached Tremont Place before they ran into Jack Cudahy, the meatpacking heir and a balloon-flying friend of von Phul's. The four men set out

Tony von Phul's angry note to Frank Henwood. Numbers are for trial exhibits. (The Denver Times, June 27, 1911. Courtesy of the Colorado Historical Society)

to tour the city's "thirst emporiums" and "smartest boozerinos" and to conduct extensive research on the products von Phul peddled for his employer, the Ruinart Wine Company.

About the time von Phul headed off for a night on the town, Henwood left the hotel to plead his case to Hamilton Armstrong, the city's police chief. His demands were simple: He wanted von Phul run out of town before someone wound up dead.

"Do you know Tony von Phul?" Henwood asked the chief.

"I've heard of him."

Without naming Isabel Springer, Henwood explained that von Phul was holding some letters from "a dear friend," letters that would be damaging to her marriage. If, he asked Armstrong, he couldn't get the letters back, would he at least see that von Phul left town? "I want the son of a bitch run out of town!"

Armstrong was having none of it. "As far as I know, von Phul has done nothing that would justify his being run out of town. I have no authority over the letters."

Frustrated, Henwood played his trump card, telling the chief that the unnamed woman was the wife of John

Springer, and that he feared that Springer would take violent steps against von Phul if something weren't done.

Armstrong was unreceptive, especially after Henwood spilled the name of the "dear friend." Springer was a powerful man with powerful friends in Denver city government, and dragging his name into the public eye would do no one, especially the chief, any good. "Mrs. Springer don't have to see Mr. von Phul if she don't want to. I think Mr. Springer is able and capable of looking after his own family affairs. Mr. Springer is the man for his wife to appeal to."

"Chief, I don't want Mr. Springer to know anything about this. John is a prominent man here. I know how much he thinks of his wife, and I realize if this man carries out his threats and gives those letters to John one by one, John will kill him."

"You should talk to Mr. Springer about that."

"Chief, isn't there something that could be done to Mr. von Phul?"

"No, not unless Mrs. Springer is willing to make a complaint and appear in court. If she is, I will arrest Mr. von Phul and unless she does, I cannot. Now, I could send for Mr. von Phul and have a talk with him. But it's optional whether he will come or not."

Henwood then spoke words that would haunt him. "If he sends those letters to Springer, I'll beat John to it—I'll kill the bastard myself."

Still Armstrong demurred. "If Mrs. Springer will swear out a complaint against von Phul, I will arrest von Phul and force him to behave or leave the city. Otherwise, there is nothing I can do."

Henwood, frustrated in his attempt to have von Phul run out of town, hurried back to the hotel. Waiting for him in the lobby was his theater party, consisting of the Springers, Isabel Springer's mother, and Henwood's business partner and friend, Frank Loveland. They were headed to a private box for the vaudeville show at the Orpheum Theater at Fifteenth and Welton Streets. When Henwood arrived to gather his theater companions at the foot of the grand staircase on the east side of the lobby, he saw, to his dismay, von Phul, trying to shanghai his guests by telling them, "You had better change your mind and come to the Broadway Theater with me."

Anxious to avoid another confrontation, Henwood smiled and said to his guests, "Are you ready to go?" Von Phul simply glared. With that, the five theatergoers were off to the Orpheum to see a bill that included a dramatic offering by actor Burr McIntosh, starring in *The Ranchman*—"one of those cheap, gun-playing romances," sniffed the critic in *The Denver Post*. Ironically, it was about two men and a woman sharing a night in a lonely Wyoming ranch house. Also on the bill were Mlle. Bianci Froehlich, offering "her repertory of classical and novelty dancing"; trapeze artist Aleide Capitaine; and The Fry Twins, a pair of wrestling brothers.

During the performance at the Orpheum, Henwood was surprised to look across the theater and see von Phul and another man, probably Cooke, seated in a box near the stage. He was even more surprised minutes later when von Phul's hand suddenly thrust through the curtains in Henwood's private box and clutched Isabel's arm. Startled, she asked to be excused to get a drink of water. Henwood and her husband prevailed on her to stay. The rest of the night passed without incident.

❖

Recognizing at last the forces she had set in motion, Isabel looked for ways to defuse things. Early in the morning of May 24, she took von Phul on a drive to the ranch with her mother, despite being assaulted by him just the day before. Later in the day, Henwood visited the Springers' rooms, where Isabel poured out the tale of her violent encounters with von Phul—though she failed to mention the drive to Henwood or to her husband. Despite her plea that Henwood get back her letters, Isabel, fearing von Phul's temper was out of control, now asked Henwood to withdraw from her affairs. "Please drop this now where you are, for my own sake, my husband's and my future. You are not dealing with this in the right way."

"You're making a mistake," he answered. "You don't know how to manage such affairs. It takes a man to handle it, man to man. Promise me you won't go near von Phul. You're making a mistake not calling for a showdown."

"I will not promise not to see him again."

"Well, then, I wash my hands of the whole thing. I've spoken to Chief Armstrong."

Isabel became angry. "You shouldn't have done that! I don't want my affairs taken to court. He knows John and will certainly tell him about this."

"No, he won't. I told him I was speaking to him man to man. He won't go to John."

They spoke for some time, but Isabel would not promise she would stay away from von Phul.

"Please, Frank, just drop it."

But there was no turning back. Not for Henwood, not for von Phul.

Isabel wrote a letter that her maid delivered to Henwood's office in the Continental Building at Sixteenth and Lawrence on the morning of May 24. Again, she warned him to stay away from her apartments at the hotel, that von Phul had threatened to kill him if he saw him with Isabel. The messenger maid told Henwood that Isabel and von Phul had argued "all afternoon" the previous day.

❖

After he received Isabel's note, Henwood, the man who believed anyone who carried a gun was a coward and who had never owned a weapon, took the precaution of stopping at a hardware store near the Daniels & Fisher department store, where he purchased an old five-shot, .38-caliber Smith & Wesson pearl-handled revolver and a box of cartridges. He was ready if von Phul decided to come after him.

About six that evening, Isabel hurried to Henwood's room to repeat her warnings that von Phul had threatened to "fix him." Again she urged him to let her take care of the situation.

Henwood immediately called Chief Armstrong at home. "Mrs. Springer has just left my room. Isn't there something that can be done?"

"No. If Mrs. Springer is being molested and she is willing to appear in court against Mr. von Phul I will arrest him."

"That can't be done. If I call Mrs. Springer to the telephone, will you talk to her and advise her what to do?"

"I have no advice to give her. If she has got into a difficulty she got into it without any advice of mine and she will have to get out of it without any advice of mine. I will have nothing to do with this affair."

That evening, Henwood and some acquaintances trooped across Broadway to see a performance of Flo Ziegfeld's *Follies of 1910* at the Broadway Theater in the Hotel Metropole. *Follies*, a musical sensation starring comedian Bert Williams, Lillian Lorraine, Fannie Brice, and "75 Anna Held show girls," drew glowing reviews in the local newspapers. Among the novelties was the opening scene in which chorus girls marched through the audience from the back of the theater. Lorraine sang "Swing Me High, Swing Me Low" while she sailed back and forth over the stage on a swing. The *Rocky Mountain News* critic raved, "It would bankrupt the English language to tell adequately of the wonderful conglomeration of mirth, music, beauty, scenic effects and theatrical knick-knacks that go to make up this charming 'revue' prepared by Ziegfeld, the wizard."

The previous Sunday's opening performance had been packed with members of Denver society. The Springers had attended, accompanied by Henwood, his friend Frank Loveland, and Isabel's actress friend Louise Cherry. Also in the audience were Mayor Robert W. Speer and his wife and many of the city's leading businessmen. Isabel was described by an observer as "one of the most strikingly beautiful women in the house." Springer, in particular, seemed charmed by the show's bathing-beauty scene in which ten chorines peeled down to knee-length, one-piece bathing suits for a day at the beach. Springer became so enamored that he had to be restrained by friends from toppling out of his box as he leaned forward for a closer view.

Three nights later, as the curtain rose again on *Follies*, it also was about to rise on one of the most sensational murders in the city's history. When the performance ended near 11:15 P.M., Henwood recrossed the wide Broadway thoroughfare and entered the east side of the hotel at almost the same moment as Tony von Phul, who also had been at *Follies*. Each man, perhaps knowing what he would find, headed toward his mutual fate.

Chapter Two
THE SHOOTING: "I WAS READY FOR HIM"

IT WAS COMING UP MIDNIGHT and men, laughing and talking loudly, crowded into the bar a few steps off the lobby of the Brown Palace. The intimate barroom next to the hotel's Broadway entrance was almost full; it always was when the Broadway Theater let out.

Less than ten minutes after *Follies of 1910* ended, about 11:15 P.M. on May 24, 1911, Frank Henwood found his way into the Wine Room, also known as the Marble Bar for its exquisite front bar covered with pale golden onyx imported from Mexico, the same material used in the lobby and on the massive fireplace mantel near the Seventeenth Street entrance.

Henwood was no stranger to the barroom, which he visited frequently after moving into the seventh floor of the Brown while pursuing well-to-do investors for his employer. As he entered, Henwood scanned the assemblage for a familiar face, then approached the center of the bar, near the beer taps, and joined three men—A. C. Rollestone, vice president of the Victor Bank in the Colorado mountain mining town of Victor; retired Judge James Owen of Colorado Springs; and Charles Schilling, a dealer in dry goods in Victor, all of whom had been at the *Follies* performance.

That Owen and Henwood were still speaking was something of a surprise. The two met earlier in the evening when they were seated next to each other in Rollestone's box at the theater. Shortly after they were introduced, Henwood, a man

25

for whom formalities were time wasted, smacked the judge on the shoulder, pointed to the stage, where the girls of *Follies* bounded about, and said, "Take your choice, old boy, and I'll get her for you after the show is over." Owen was not amused and told Henwood so. But after the two men met in the barroom, Henwood apologized. "I didn't mean anything, old chap. You just don't understand our free and easy Western ways."

"Not your kind of Western ways, I'll admit," said Owen. But he added, "Forget it," and they shook hands.

As they chatted, Henwood ordered a bottle of champagne for the foursome. The other three declined, so he chose a small bottle for himself.

Minutes later, Tony von Phul arrived, accompanied by Ed "Pop" Rosenbaum, manager of the touring *Follies* company. Von Phul had become familiar with the *Follies* cast and management the previous summer during its run in New York City, where he was often seen backstage and where he showered his attentions on numerous members of the chorus line. He stepped to the bar and ordered a glass of whiskey and a beer. Noting von Phul's arrival, Henwood excused himself and walked back to the Broadway Theater to find Frank Darling, the musical director of the stage company, who had planned to join Henwood at the bar. Unsuccessful in locating Darling, Henwood rejoined his companions in less than five minutes.

Like pieces in a deadly game of chess, the players rearranged themselves along the bar. At first, Rosenbaum stood with von Phul to his left and Henwood on his right. Von Phul, still steaming from two days of nasty encounters with Henwood, commented to Rosenbaum, loud enough for others to hear, "There's that son of a bitch I licked, and I ought to lick him again." He leaned close to Rosenbaum and asked him to switch places, putting von Phul within five feet of his rival. Von Phul offered to send a bottle of wine up to

The Marble Bar at the Brown Palace Hotel, scene of the May 24, 1911, shooting. (Courtesy of the Denver Public Library, Western History Department)

Rosenbaum's wife. The theater manager left to see if she were still awake, promising to return.

Henwood spoke first. "Tony…I mean, Mr. von Phul," he said, correcting himself because he knew how much the St. Louisan hated the familiarity. "Won't you reconsider what happened yesterday afternoon?"

Von Phul looked at him, then told Henwood, "I'm going upstairs and I am going to grab that gray-headed son of a bitch by the hair and pull him out of there and show him who is master here." Both men knew he was talking about Springer, the husband of their mutual interest.

Henwood bristled. "You can't get that over on me."

Those standing closest to the two men tensed. James W. Atkinson, a portly, white-haired, fifty-five-year-old Colorado Springs contractor who had stopped for a quick drink before catching the midnight train home, commented to those with him, "Let's get out of here, there is going to be a fight."

Von Phul, his eyes fixed on Henwood, snarled, "I will get you first." He lashed out, landing a sharp backhand right to the point of Henwood's jaw. Surprised by the suddenness of the blow, Henwood staggered backward and landed hard on the seat of his pants, striking his head on the marble floor.

Stunned, and convinced that von Phul, who had struck him and stuck a weapon in his midsection the previous day, meant to pull a gun on him, the terrified Henwood rose to one knee and struggled to jerk his newly purchased revolver from his hip pocket. The gun hung up momentarily. "He's going to shoot!" someone shouted as Henwood, now on his feet, opened fire. There were two quick shots, then a pause, followed by three more shots in rapid succession. For a man with no experience handling a gun, Henwood's aim was tragically accurate. That his target was less than ten feet away enhanced his aim.

What happened in the seconds between the time von Phul knocked Henwood to the floor and the entrepreneur came up firing is clouded in controversy. Henwood would stand trial in 1911 and 1913 for the shooting, but witnesses, of which there were plenty, could not agree on a key issue. Some swore von Phul was facing Henwood when the first shot was fired; others were just as certain von Phul had turned to the bar and had taken the first bullet in the back.

Henwood maintained that after he was knocked down, von Phul fixed him with what he called "a look of hate and threat." Some bystanders said that von Phul appeared to reach for his right hip pocket and many of them, especially Henwood, assumed, a pistol, perhaps the one with which he had threatened Henwood.

Henwood's first shot struck von Phul in the right shoulder, causing him to lurch forward, exposing to Henwood's blazing .38 another patron standing at the bar, George E. Copeland, forty-three-year-old proprietor of an ore-sampling works in Victor. Von Phul tried to escape the barrage

*George E. Copeland, the second
victim of the shooting. (*The
Denver Post, *June 1, 1911.
Courtesy of the Colorado
Historical Society)*

by crouching down and scuttling along the bar, seeking
refuge in the adjacent smoking lounge. The next two bullets
hit Copeland, who had just asked the bartender for a gin
rickey, in the right hip and the left thigh, cutting the
femoral artery.

In a frenzy, Henwood kept squeezing the trigger as twenty
or so patrons scrambled for cover. His fourth shot passed
through von Phul's upraised right wrist and hit Atkinson in
the left thigh, shattering his femur. "My God! I'm shot!"
Atkinson exclaimed as he hopped two or three steps, then
sank to the floor near the door to the lobby.

It was Henwood's fifth shot that proved fatal for the burly
St. Louis aeronaut. As von Phul tried to reach the bar's entrance
and safety, a bullet pierced his left side between the eleventh
and twelfth ribs, coursed upward through his body, grazed his
stomach, and lodged under the skin on his abdomen.

Henwood jerked the trigger again and again, but his
efforts produced only hollow clicks. Finally, Frank Canfield,

who worked in the hotel as an elevator operator, ripped the gun from his hand and placed it on the bar. Bartender Frank Miller picked it up and put it in a drawer.

Smoke and silence filled the small barroom. In the pandemonium that followed, Copeland lay on the floor near the end of the bar, and Atkinson, a cigar clinched in his teeth, was lying partly across the barroom entrance. Dazed but strangely calm, Henwood casually picked up his straw hat and walked toward the lobby. As he passed the prostrate Atkinson, he paused and said, "I'm sorry I shot you. Can I help you?" Atkinson snapped, "You've done enough already. Get out and leave me alone." He added an epithet or two for emphasis.

The mortally wounded von Phul fell into a plush leather chair in a small room next to the bar. Blood poured freely from his right wrist. He used his left hand to hold his right arm in the air. Those who reached him first heard him say, "Get a doctor quickly. I am very badly hurt."

A crowd gathered around him. Some, including Henwood's attorney, would claim that it was at this moment that von Phul's weapon disappeared from his possession. Among

*A newspaper depiction of how Tony von Phul and George E. Copeland were shot by Frank Henwood. (*The Denver Post, *June 22, 1911. Courtesy of the Colorado Historical Society)*

those ministering to von Phul was a young musician from the *Follies* orchestra, Denver native Paul Whiteman, later to become a noted leader of his own jazz orchestra. Whiteman saw that von Phul was in danger of bleeding to death. Quickly, he searched von Phul's pockets for a handkerchief with which to stop the flow. He found one in the right coat pocket and tied it around the wounded man's wrist. Then he took his own handkerchief and applied it to the wound in von Phul's shoulder. What he did not find, or feel, was a gun.

The Brown Palace physician, Dr. Alfred Mann, worked to dress von Phul's wounds. As he regained his composure, von Phul sought to reassure those around him. "I'm all right, boys. That fellow winged me in the wrist and it hurts. I don't think I'm seriously injured, and I wish some of you would wire my father in St. Louis that I'm all right and not to pay any attention to the newspaper reports he reads."

Unaware of the animosity between Henwood and von Phul, the half dozen men surrounding him were puzzled by the suddenness of the violence. Von Phul had an explanation. "We had a little argument and Henwood insulted me. I knocked him down and he came up shooting. The attack was cowardly in the extreme. I was not armed and Henwood must have known I was not. He is in luck. If I had had a gun, he would have got as good as he sent."

Von Phul chatted with Dr. Mann as the latter tended to him. Then, as if dimly aware of the seriousness of his worsening condition, he reeled off a series of names of those who should be notified if he died.

Dr. Mann told von Phul he needed to go to a hospital.

"Get me a taxicab, if you're bound to take me to the hospital. I don't think it's worthwhile going to the hospital. Why can't I go to my room, doctor?"

"A hotel room is no place for a wounded man."

"It's good enough for me. What's the matter with all of you? Let me alone."

Rosenbaum, the *Follies* manager with whom he had been sharing a drink at the bar minutes earlier, pleaded, "Be reasonable, Tony."

"I am reasonable."

Suddenly, he looked around. "Who's got my watch?" A friend held it out and he caught it. "I want that watch, and I want everything else that belongs to me."

"You've got everything, Tony," Rosenbaum comforted.

"All right."

He put on his coat and walked outside to Broadway, where he saw the police ambulance backed up to the curb. The man who had survived numerous close calls as a balloonist refused to ride in it.

"Not me for the ambulance."

"Tony, here's a taxi if you wish," said one of his friends.

"Me for the taxi." Accompanied by police surgeon Dr. Willis Mudd and two friends, he rode to St. Luke's Hospital like a warrior leaving the field of battle.

❖

Henwood made no attempt to escape. "I did it," he said, to no one in particular. "I was attacked." Appalled that he had wounded Copeland and Atkinson, Henwood broke down in tears. "I didn't mean to do it! Oh, just let me touch him. I didn't mean to do it!" He sat quietly on a couch in the lobby until policeman Leonard Anderson, attracted by the sound of shots as he walked past the hotel, came upon him and placed him under arrest. Moments later, Chief Hamilton Armstrong and detectives Peter Carr and Timothy Connor took Henwood into custody.

The police carted him off to jail at City Hall, at Fourteenth and Larimer Streets. An architectural pile of stone and peculiar features, City Hall squatted like a gargoyle beside Cherry Creek, its basement cells a haven for rats. Once at the jail, Chief Armstrong asked his prisoner what prompted the shooting.

"Von Phul was looking for trouble and found it. He was after me for some time, but I was ready for him." He repeated his repulsion for gunplay. "I never carried a gun in my life until tonight but I was told that von Phul always carried weapons and was a bad man, and I thought I would take steps to protect myself."

He didn't reveal what triggered the incident. "We had a few words while standing at the bar. His attitude angered me and I may have used strong language. He struck me and I protected myself with my revolver." He showed no regret, except that he had winged two bystanders with his wild shots. "I am sorry that innocent persons were injured," he told Chief Armstrong. "I did not intend to hurt anyone but von Phul and I have no regret for having injured him, nor will I ever have."

It was nearly 2 A.M. when Henwood struck up what became a peculiar, almost friendly, relationship with reporters from the city's newspapers. Standing in the jail's hallway, he talked openly in an impromptu press conference. He was not completely honest, however, preferring to concoct fanciful tales rather than revealing the true cause of the fracas. "I am sorry that I cannot tell you fellows just what prompted the shooting; but, really, I have forgotten what it was. You may say that he liked the bathing girls with the 'Follies' company, that I disagreed with him and that we had words which led to blows and then to the shooting."

Other stories were brought up: that wine salesman von Phul belittled Henwood for his choice of vintages in the barroom the night of the shooting and ordered the bartender to bring a different bottle, one from his employer's line; or that he may have called von Phul a liar. He couldn't recall.

Asked why he was carrying a gun, Henwood shrugged and joked, "Oh, I have a trunk full of revolvers in my room. I've been collecting them. I have some from Mexico, some from India and some from the South Pole. Each has a pedigree."

A reporter asked, "Had you ever met von Phul previous to your first meeting in Denver?" Henwood paused, then said, "I don't think I care to answer that question. I have said all I care to say and you can roll your little hoop." With that he walked toward his cell.

As he entered the small room, he turned and said, "Tell them Tony von Phul stuck his finger in my wine, and it made me sore. That started the fight."

"Is that your reason for killing a man?"

"That's my answer."

When he awoke the next morning after a night of sound sleep, Henwood asked jailers for the morning papers "to see how many bouquets the reporters threw at me."

❖

At St. Luke's Hospital, only a few blocks east of the hotel, von Phul was getting bad news.

"How bad are my wounds, doctor?"

"They are fatal," Dr. Van Dyck McKelvey responded.

"How long will I live?"

"Oh, I think until about noon."

With only hours to live, the man *The Denver Post* characterized as "the connoisseur of life's pleasures…a sporting man, free, easy, unmarried" tried to put his life in order. He told one of his nurses, "Well, I've been close to death about fifty times when ballooning, but the doctor says it is going to come this time at noon. Well, I always said I would never get killed ballooning, and this settles that."

Doctors wanted to operate to remove the bullet in his abdomen, but before he would let them, von Phul asked that a priest be sent to his room. It was to Father McDonough that he unburdened himself of the real causes of the barroom tragedy. With everyone else, he declined to discuss the woman in the case, other than to tell a nurse, "I hold no grudge against Henwood. He was a good sport, but I didn't think he'd let a woman come between us. He insulted me and I knocked him down just as I would any cur. I did not think for a moment that he would shoot. When he got up he started shooting. The coward fired five shots at me while I stood there helpless. The first bullet entered my right shoulder and left me completely at the mercy of the dog."

Fred Cooke, the cousin with whom he had shared dinner at the Brown Palace the night before, said, "My God, Tony, what was the trouble? Was it that woman?"

"For God's sake, don't talk about it. Can't you see I'm a goner?"

He told Cooke, "Henwood was a fool for making so much of a fuss over one woman." As his life ebbed, von Phul's mind wandered and his conversation rambled, mainly about his ballooning adventures. He asked one of his nurses for oxygen. "I remember the time I was nearly killed when [actress] Eva Tanguay was a passenger. That was home in St. Louis. I never thought about the parachute which always I carried for protection, and the boys had neglected to attach it. We were up a thousand feet before I noticed it. As luck would have it, the gas began to leak, we had to throw everything overboard in the way of ballast, and managed to alight all right." He recalled other narrow escapes in his balloon and lamented that he would be unable to make a planned flight over Pikes Peak with his friend Jack Cudahy.

As he slipped nearer death, his conversation became incoherent, although one of the nurses said she thought he talked more about his ballooning adventures.

Near 10 A.M., Deputy District Attorney Edgar McComb, policeman William A. Dollison, and Chief Armstrong arrived at St. Luke's Hospital to take von Phul's testimony on the incident. However, von Phul's situation was so critical they couldn't talk with him without a doctor's permission, and attending physician W. W. Grant was away from the hospital. The trio was forced to wait outside von Phul's room for more than an hour before Dr. Grant returned.

The three men started into von Phul's room, but a nurse stepped out and said, "He's dead." It was 11:20 A.M., almost exactly twelve hours since the shooting.

A coroner's inquest the following day was quick and to the point. After fifteen minutes of deliberation, the jury, composed of Frank D. Meek, E. H. Cumbe, H. J. Gebhart, W. H. Cavanaugh, Henry Kachel, and John Moran, found:

> That the said Sylvester L. von Phul came to his death by gunshot wounds having been fired by Frank H. Henwood in the City and County of Denver in the state of Colorado about 11:35 P.M. on Wednesday, May 24, 1911, in the barroom of the Brown Palace Hotel at Seventeenth and Broadway; and we further find the said Sylvester L. von Phul died at St. Luke's Hospital about 11:30 A.M. May 25, 1911, and we further find that said shots were fired with felonious intent.

Just after midnight on June 1, 1911, Copeland, the unlucky bystander who had stopped two bullets, followed Tony von Phul in death at St. Luke's Hospital. He succumbed after doctors amputated his left leg because they couldn't control the hemorrhaging.

With the two men's deaths, Henwood's claim of self-defense was doomed.

Chapter Three

Tony von Phul: "An Awful Mess"

Tony von Phul was the kind of man other men liked to be around.

He took risks, possessed more than his share of self-confidence, and was a rough-and-ready adventurer. His given name was Sylvester Louis von Phul, fine for a man of comfortable background, which he was, but hardly apt for a dashing young man—some said a bounder—whose passions included ranching, racing horses and cars, soaring in balloons and, to a great extent, romancing beautiful and, sometimes, married women. "Tony" fit him better.

He was born in St. Louis in 1878, the youngest of six children, into a well-known St. Louis family said to be related to Pierre Laclede, one of the city's founders. His father, Frederick, was an official with the city's street department. Von Phul grew up in middle-class surroundings and attended public schools, where he may have been a childhood friend of Isabel Patterson.

After a four-year scientific course he was graduated in 1895 from Christian Brothers College High School, where he was a star baseball and football player. He launched a promising and profitable career in a St. Louis brokerage office but lasted only five years before his restless nature took hold. Unable to be constrained by a desk job, he set out for the Bar L Ranch near the town of Coalridge in the Indian Territory, where he learned to "ride, rope and muster the horse."

*Tony von Phul. (*Rocky Mountain News,
May 26, 1911. Courtesy of the
Colorado Historical Society)

By 1903, he was back in St. Louis and becoming a note-worthy jockey. At one point, he won a steeplechase by fifteen lengths on a horse called Mrs. Grannon, and in 1904 he won three of five events at the city's premier horse show. He followed that up by winning ten of fifteen races he entered as a "gentleman jockey" against other amateur racers in 1906.

A glowing profile of the successful young man, based largely on his family connections, appeared in *The St. Louis Republic* in 1909. "Von Phul is poor of purse," it noted. "He has been earning his living these many years. He was born handicapped with a name which spelled wealth, ancestry and affluence. But this mattered not to him."

He seemed to know no fear. "He from very boyhood had lived in a whirlpool of thrills, of dangerous excitement. He spoke not in the spirit of bravado. He seems to know not what nerves are; what it is to chill; neither does he become enthusiastic. He would have made a champion prize fighter."

Life on the ranch had toughened the strapping young man. He was good with his fists and harbored a temper that led him to use them frequently. One night, while returning to St. Louis, he was stopped by two highwaymen at a bridge approach to the city. "Two glittering guns were thrust at his head. With a well-directed blow he knocked one of the robbers down, after which he went after the other one. He succeeded in disarming him, after which he beat him up severely and then took him to the East Side police station." He could be on the other side of the law as well and was known to have a violent temper when drinking. In one well-publicized brawl with a policeman, he had three teeth shot out.

In 1908, von Phul experienced the kind of epiphany that comes to young men craving adventure—he discovered ballooning, a pastime that fit his demeanor. An aggressive and fearless pilot, his cap turned backward to enhance his already heroic appearance, he escaped death a number of times while soaring over the Midlands.

Ballooning became his passion. His first ride, on December 6, 1908, with a friend, Captain H. E. Honeywell, as pilot, made him a confirmed flyer. As he did with other pursuits, von Phul became proficient, "one of the best pilots in St. Louis," said one observer. On their flight, Honeywell and von Phul drifted as high as 6,700 feet and landed in Willisville, Illinois, three hours after liftoff from Second and Rutger Streets in St. Louis. He qualified as a pilot in 1909 and was made a member of the Aero Club of St. Louis, one of the nation's largest such groups. St. Louis was a center of American balloonists, and the Aero Club boasted four hundred members. Only Cincinnati and Chicago could claim as many enthusiasts. Von Phul was a leader among the Aero Club's fliers. In 1909, he won the club's silver trophy for a 548-mile trip.

Death, or at least the possibility of it, was no stranger to him. Preparing to launch his balloon one day, his helpers

Tony von Phul, right, in balloon with an unidentified man, circa 1908. (Courtesy of the Missouri Historical Society)

released the balloon just as he was stepping into the basket. The balloon and its scrambling passenger shot into the air. Only quick action allowed him to grab a guy rope and pull himself into the car.

Women were frequent passengers. In 1910, he was accompanied by actress Gertrude Hoffman, a beauty who appeared with numerous versions of the *Ziegfeld Follies*. As von Phul and Hoffman lifted off, she began singing at the top of her voice "I Don't Care," a racy ditty of the day made popular by Ziegfeld star and another von Phul sailing companion, Eva Tanguay. "[It] could be heard until she was several hundred feet in the air." Even if she didn't care, the duo landed safely in Illinois.

In 1909, von Phul, his status among the ballooning crowd growing, and Maj. Albert Bond Lambert, another noted aeronaut, sailed from St. Louis to Ridgeville, South Carolina, 685 miles away, in fifteen hours and twenty-nine minutes.

Their takeoff from St. Louis on October 15 did not portend a safe flight. "The ascent was one of the most dangerous ever witnessed at the gasworks, owing to the puffy wind," the *St. Louis Globe-Democrat* noted in a front-page story. Only quick work by the two aeronauts, who dumped two-and-a-half bags of ballast, allowed them to clear telegraph wires by twenty feet at one end of the takeoff zone. En route to South Carolina, the men narrowly averted a crash in the Cumberland Mountains of Tennessee when clouds parted suddenly to reveal a large mountain in their path. Dumping ballast allowed them to rise over the obstacle. At one point, the balloon, clocked at speeds up to seventy-four miles an hour, rose to 12,400 feet where temperatures fell to minus six degrees.

Lambert recalled in a 1928 reminiscence,

We left St. Louis at 6:30 P.M. and landed near Charleston, South Carolina, the next morning at 8 A.M. Shortly after daylight, we saw the ocean from an altitude of fourteen thousand feet. We had to come down in a hurry. We struck the top of the last tree with high tide ahead. I managed to hang on but Tony fell into a large bramble bush. The news of our flight preceded us. After a rough wagon ride we reached Charleston to be greeted by the Chamber of Commerce, which organized a luncheon in our honor. Von Phul mysteriously disappeared and was not to be found in spite of a diligent search. About 4 P.M. he made his appearance. "Where have you been?" was asked by a large crowd gathered around. "Down in the Turkish bath, having the thorns pulled out," he said.

It was with Wooster Lambert, a St. Louis millionaire and Albert's younger brother, that von Phul had another of his brushes with death in 1910. Lambert, a first-time flier, and von Phul lifted off in St. Louis III at 9:45 A.M. "As the big aerostat shot upward," reported *The St. Louis Republic*, "young Lambert kept his eyes toward the sky as if to see if they were going to hit a cloud, although Mrs. Albert Bond Lambert,

Mrs. Marion Lambert and Miss Jane Blackwell tried to get his attention long enough to wave goodbye."

The two men were riding comfortably at eight thousand feet when clouds caused the balloon's gas to cool, leading the rig to drop to four thousand feet before they could dump ballast and rise back to eight thousand. Von Phul discovered that the line regulating the gas supply had become entangled, and the basket began to slowly sink toward the Mississippi, finally hitting the water a hundred yards offshore.

"There was nothing for us to do," von Phul told a reporter. "We were entirely helpless. Of course, we threw every pound of weight over but we came down faster and faster. It would be hard to describe our feelings, neither of us expecting to ever escape alive. But luck seemed to be with us, for like a plummet we dropped into the Mississippi River." A passing launch towed them to shore. *The Republic* mockingly described the journey as "a record for slow speed, having consumed two and a half hours to cover six miles."

By 1911, von Phul had logged more than fifty flights, including participation in the world-famous 1909 International, during which he and aide Joseph O'Reilly flew seven hundred miles from St. Louis to Wahkon, Minnesota, winning the Centennial race and apparently winning the Lahm Cup. They were disqualified from the latter because von Phul failed to pay the one-dollar entry. He paid for his ballooning habit, which cost him one hundred dollars every time he lifted off, by working as a representative of the Anheuser-Busch brewery and, later, as a salesman for a champagne and wine distributor. He was eager to take a trip in the adventurer's new toy, the aeroplane. The club was planning to purchase one of the Wright Brothers' flying machines, and von Phul pronounced the idea of powered flight was "exactly what I have been waiting for."

It wasn't about money. The handsome, risk-taking flier was in it for the thrills. *The Republic* trumpeted of him, "If Von Phul was possessed of the spirit of hysteria—one who courted publicity just for the sensation of reading his laudations, or was one who danced before the public in order to further his interests, the story of his life, battles and career would not be worth the thought. In all his deeds, all his triumphs and his successes on the track, in the arena, in the air, in fact, everywhere he has profited little."

Von Phul's bachelorhood and reputation as an aeronaut and ladies' man made him a favorite among the young set in St. Louis. He was a frequent visitor at the graceful and stylish Jefferson Hotel, planned as an office building but built as a hotel, the city's first with air conditioning, to accommodate the crush of visitors to the World's Fair in 1904. The hotel's massive Gold Room could hold a thousand revelers, and often did. It was the center of downtown life. "At midnight, things begin to wake up," noted a local society writer, and rows of limousines dropped off well-to-do fun seekers who would dine and dance into the wee hours.

❖

Von Phul and the newly divorced Isabel Patterson Folck were familiar faces at the Gold Room. He pursued her ardently until she chose to marry John Springer and depart St. Louis for a new life in Denver. Her marriage, however, did not diminish his interest in her, nor hers in him. She visited St. Louis often and they would see each other from time to time. Beginning in January 1911, she wrote him that series of passionate and pleading letters, promising him her devotion "with all the love a woman is able to give" and beseeching him to be by her side. He heeded her pleadings and arrived in the Queen City on May 23, 1911. He and his rival, Frank Henwood, almost immediately became locked in a series of clashes over the letters, culminating in the May 24 barroom showdown at the Brown Palace and von Phul's death on May 25.

Both Henwood and von Phul attempted to keep Mrs. Springer's name out of the case and out of the public prints. It was futile. Her picture appeared in a Denver newspaper the day after the shooting, and there were numerous reports that the fight was over an unnamed society woman. Henwood concocted a story that the two men had quarreled over the quality of one of von Phul's employer's vintages. For his part, von Phul claimed that he was in Denver to set up a balloon crossing of Pikes Peak with his friend, Jack Cudahy, the Kansas City meatpacker.

In the days immediately following the shooting, von Phul's friends and relatives rushed to his defense, insisting that he didn't pack a weapon and that he was the possessor of a controlled disposition. His brother-in-law, Joseph Murphy, told the Denver district attorney's office, "Mr. von Phul was not a barroom fighter or drunkard, and his friends are determined that his memory shall not live in the public mind as having met his end in a barroom brawl." The incident at the Brown readily fit that description. Murphy hinted that the shooting "was the result of a carefully worked out conspiracy, hatched in St. Louis and carried out at a place where the murderer would have tremendous and interested wealth behind him."

Murphy even went so far as to say that his brother-in-law "has not carried a weapon for two years." He noted, "When Tony was younger, he spent some time on a ranch in the Southwest and there he formed the habit of carrying a revolver. When he returned to St. Louis, I had a talk with him and convinced him it was a certain way to get into trouble in a city. He agreed with me and put the weapon away. Since then I know he has not carried a revolver."

If von Phul didn't carry a weapon, it had a habit of following him around during his brief stay at the Brown Palace. The whereabouts of his revolver was one of the key bits of evidence in Henwood's first trial. Von Phul had three different rooms at the Brown and twice left his pistol behind, to be picked up by the maid who was moving his luggage to his new room. Ultimately, the weapon was turned over to the clerk at the front desk and locked in the hotel's safe the night before the barroom showdown.

Although his family insisted that von Phul didn't carry a gun, Mrs. Corinne Johnson Swan, a Denver socialite, disagreed. She knew von Phul briefly in St. Louis and was supposed to testify at Henwood's first trial, but was scared off by an anonymous phone call that warned, "If you dare go on the witness stand in the Henwood case, you'll regret it." She found von Phul boastful and arrogant, although she hastened to make clear that the two of them "were never more than friends." Shortly before Henwood's 1913 trial, she told *The Denver Post,*

> Von Phul was always boastful when drinking. I never heard him threaten to kill anyone or anything like that but I always gathered that perhaps he might not hesitate to shoot if in a temper when drinking. One night at the Planters [Hotel in St. Louis] after he had taken a glass or two too much, he shifted his revolver from one pocket to another. He was seated next to me. I asked him point blank why he should go about armed. [He said,] "I'm never dressed until I have my gun on me—I need it in my business."

Tony's cousin, Henry von Phul, a former sheriff in Cripple Creek, Colorado, was sure it was a murder plot. "I believe it was a plain case of murder. My investigations go to show that Henwood is a bad man. He was looking for trouble. Our family does not relish the idea of scandal nor are we looking for it, but this affair is going to be probed to the bottom."

As he lay dying, with only a few hours of life remaining, von Phul declined to name the woman in the case, other than to say of his assailant, "This is an awful mess to make over a woman." He preferred to regale his nurses with stories of his ballooning exploits. "It is too bad this thing happened," he said shortly before he lapsed into unconsciousness about an hour before he died. "I had arranged for a flight in Kansas City on July 5. I hoped to make a new record." The race was preliminary to that fall's International race where von Phul was scheduled to represent the Aero Club of St. Louis. It was not to be. His last words to his nurses were, "Well, if that fellow has put the quietus on me, I'll die game."

As death crept over him, he remained calm. Clyde MacKinley, stage manager for the *Follies of 1910*, who had known von Phul for almost a decade, recalled, "He knew he was badly hurt but he never showed a bit of fear. He was the gamest man I ever knew. He knew he was going to die— I know from some of the things he said to me. For one thing,

The coroner attributed Tony von Phul's death to "gun shot wounds." (Dick Kreck collection)

he said, 'I wish I could get well, just to get even with that fellow in my own way. Maybe he can get away with it, but he oughtn't.'"

After his death, von Phul's body was claimed by his cousin Henry, then taken by train to Kansas City where it was met by two of his closest friends, Dewey Hickey and Charles Michel, who accompanied it to St. Louis. The aeronaut's funeral at New Cathedral Chapel on May 29 was one of the city's largest, attracting three thousand mourners. Despite being desperately ill, von Phul's ailing seventy-eight-year-old father, Frederick, insisted on keeping a vigil beside the casket.

Pallbearers came from von Phul's cadre of friends in ballooning and from the Hot-Time Minstrels, with whom he frequently performed. Honorary pallbearers were the six surviving founders of the Aero Club, Albert Bond Lambert, Capt. John Berry, Capt. H. E. Honeywell, Harlow Spencer, Andrew Drew, and James W. Bemis. Active pallbearers, all Hot-Time members, were Hickey, Ralph W. Coale, Clinton Boogher, H. C. Collins, Marlon Lambert, and Joseph M. O'Reilly.

The gathered throng that heard Father O'Connor's ten-minute sermon at the New Cathedral Chapel "were moved to tears" as he warned his audience of the fitfulness of life and admonished them to be prepared to meet a sudden end.

Chapter Four
FRANK HENWOOD:
"I CAN'T TRY MY CASE IN THE PAPERS"

WHAT DO YOU WANT?"
The prisoner's voice trembled as he looked over the two men entering his cell at City Jail.

"I am going to take you over to the West Side criminal court, where you are to be arraigned," answered Deputy Sheriff Henry Lewis.

Frank Henwood rose from his bunk. "I wish you'd telephone my friend, Frank Loveland; he doesn't know it."

Lewis led Henwood out of the jail to a patrol car waiting at the curb and the two men drove the eight blocks from City Jail at Fourteenth and Larimer Streets to the West Side Court building at West Colfax Avenue and Speer Boulevard, a decrepit two-story building put up in 1874 as the Arapahoe County Jail. Two tiers of cells had once occupied the back of the building. Even the windows of the sheriff's office were covered with bars. Politicians and jurors had campaigned for years to have the building replaced.

As he entered the room, Henwood recognized his attorney, John T. Bottom. Henwood turned to Lewis. "You needn't send for Loveland but I wish you'd tell him. Where will I be?"

"In the County Jail."

Looking stylish in a tailored gray suit, a shirt with a high white collar, and a dark tie, his derby tilted jauntily over his right ear and carrying a briefcase, Henwood strode into court for the first time just after 10 A.M. on June 1, 1911. Tucked

*Nattily attired Frank Henwood walks from the courtroom, followed by his attorney John T. Bottom. (*The Denver Times, *June 1, 1911. Courtesy of the Colorado Historical Society)*

under one arm was a Thermos bottle. Jammed into the left pocket of his coat were several days' editions of newspapers, ones he read faithfully to keep up with his case.

The arraignment lasted less than thirty minutes. District Attorney Willis V. Elliott charged Henwood with "the willful, deliberate and premeditated murder of one Sylvester Louis von Phul" at the Brown Palace Hotel on the night of May 24.

Speaking for his client, Bottom entered a plea of not guilty to either willful or premeditated intent to kill but admitted the killing in self-defense. He also requested that Judge Greeley W. Whitford set a time for hearing arguments for bond. Judge Whitford set the date as Saturday, two days away.

Henwood was led out of the court and taken to the warden's office in the new County Jail, separated from the courthouse by a 150-foot expanse of grass. Opened in 1891, the jail was an imposing cut-stone structure that combined the look of a cathedral and medieval castle. There, Henwood was weighed (162 pounds), then escorted to a cell.

Judge Greeley W. Whitford, circa 1930. (The Denver Post. *Courtesy of the Colorado Historical Society)*

When Loveland visited Henwood in his cell, he found his friend despondent. A second victim, mining man George Copeland, had died of two gunshot wounds during the night. Warden Patrick Riordan woke Henwood at 5 A.M. to tell him that Copeland, an uninvolved bystander, had died of loss of blood at 12:20 that morning. Henwood stared at Riordan without speaking, then flung himself down on his cot. "I will go mad!" he shouted. When Loveland arrived, Henwood was on the verge of collapse. He refused to eat, choosing instead to lie motionless on his bed. He declined to answer reporters' questions. "I can't talk to you. I can't think since I heard of Copeland's death. I can't talk. I shall go mad."

The next day, he was back in court, facing arraignment for the murder of Copeland. He now stood accused of double murder. Again he pleaded not guilty. His trial was set to begin on June 20, but Bottom immediately asked for a five-week delay. Like his request for bond, it was denied.

On Tuesday, June 20, a crowd composed mainly of women began jockeying for seats in Judge Whitford's courtroom at 7 A.M., three hours before the trial was to begin. So many tried to gain entry that once the seats in the courtroom were filled and standing room was taken, the doors were left open so the over-flow in the hallway could hear the proceedings and so some badly needed air could reach the stuffy courtroom. Attorneys for both sides lingered outside the court until past 10. Henwood waited in a side room, chatting with bystanders. "I feel fine, perfectly at ease," he said as the jail mascot, a fox terrier, played at his feet. "It's funny but it isn't bothering me at all."

Henwood, a fancier of dogs, became friends with the fox terrier shortly after he moved into his cell. The dog belonged to the warden, Riordan, but preferred Henwood's company. The animal was named Ellis Thrush Riordan, in honor of its former owner, Justice of the Peace Ellis Thrush, and E.T.R. made it his job to roam the jail halls, checking in with various prisoners; Henwood was his favorite. He frequently slept at the foot of Henwood's bunk and seemed to know when things were going badly in the courtroom. He often trailed Henwood on his walks between the jail and the courtroom. In July, E.T.R. disappeared after following his owner to a streetcar stop near the jail. He was never found, leaving Henwood alone again.

"Hear ye, hear ye," called the bailiff. The principals in the unfolding drama hurried to their places. Judge Whitford was known as a hard-line interpreter of the law. He had arrived in Denver in 1887 and became partner in a law firm that also included Platt Rogers and John F. Shafroth. He served as U. S. district attorney from 1897 to 1901 and in 1903 was a member of the convention to draw up a city charter for Denver. He also was a staunch Republican and counted John Springer among his many influential friends.

Spectators applauded when Henwood entered the room and took his chair at the defendant's table, seated directly behind Bottom and another attorney, Milner Cleaves. To his left, across the table, were prosecutors John Horne Chiles and Elliott. The jurors sat against one wall, opposite a bank of three high windows that could be opened to let some air into the courtroom. In one corner, a table was set up for reporters. The judge sat behind a large desk elevated above the proceedings and flanked on either side by lamps.

The reception for Henwood did not sit well with some. "That's like people," one guard grumped to another. "Place a man on trial for boiling his wife, and he will get notes from admiring women. Charge a man with cutting up his family into bits and cooking the flesh from the bones with acid, or have him up for marrying a dozen women and killing them all with an ax, and he will get great bunches of flowers. What is it that makes people act like that?"

Whatever it was, onlookers couldn't get enough of the defendant. Some commented on his dapper grooming. He wore a newly pressed blue suit, set off with a narrow black scarf tied under a neatly fitting turnover collar and offset by the white edge of his vest. His thinning hair was combed back and parted neatly. A spectator whispered to her friend, "He's nice looking." A reporter covering the trial was less impressed:

> He has the nose of a prizefighter and the eyes of a society woman. His eyebrows are thin and delicately curved. Above the bridge of his nose he carries the expression of an artist, below the leer of a thug. His nose is coarse, jerked at the end and flat over the nostrils. The lips are long, loose and lagging, over a heavy jaw that bunched at the corners of his mouth. Two natures look out.

If the gathered crowd expected a show, they were disappointed. Judge Whitford had gone to Iowa because of the death of his brother, and Judge Hubert L. Shattuck, sitting in for him, granted prosecutor Elliott's request that the trial be delayed one day.

As spectators filed out, Henwood hurried through the prisoner's entrance, where he was greeted by E.T.R. "Well, we got away from them, E.T.R. And they didn't bother me much, either, and they're not going to bother me much. We've got our nerve, haven't we, E.T.R.?" His path to the jail fifty yards away was blocked by a crowd of curious onlookers and photographers, and he hurried ahead of his attorney. "Hold on! Don't go so fast," said Bottom. Henwood pushed on but his progress was slowed by the dog, who kept nipping at his pant leg. He stumbled over the excited dog, then bounded up the steps and into the jailhouse.

Inside, he was confronted by a handful of reporters who wanted to question him. Heeding his attorney's advice, he declined, saying, "You know I would like to talk to you fellows if I could but it would not do at this time. I can't try my case in the papers." He did, however, shake hands all around and allow as how he was pleased to meet them.

❖

When Henwood's trial began the next day, prosecutor Elliott, regarded as a brilliant attorney with a bright political future, had a surprise for the defense. He would seek a first-degree murder conviction, not for the killing of von Phul but for the death of George Copeland, who took two bullets in the shooting. Though Henwood went on trial for shooting Copeland, the latter's name was scarcely mentioned during the trial. On the other hand, the shadows of von Phul and Isabel Springer hung over the courtroom like specters.

It has been written frequently in accounts of the scandal and the subsequent trials that the prosecution chose to try Henwood for killing Copeland instead of for the murder of von Phul to keep Isabel Springer, the woman in the case, out of the courtroom and out of the newspapers. If true, the tactic was a spectacular failure. The city's four fiercely competitive newspapers freely mixed fact and conjecture in the days leading up to the trial. *The Denver Post*, whose main headline the day after the shooting screamed AERONAUT VON PHUL SHOT TO DEATH IN BROWN PALACE; TWO WOUNDED, already was hinting at the cause, noting in the fourth paragraph of its first story, "In the early evening Henwood and von Phul quarreled over a prominent Denver society woman." On May 26, Isabel's photograph was printed on page one of *The Post*. She was identified as "a friend of Henwood and von Phul."

Henwood's explanations that the fight was over wines or the relative merits of the chorus girls in *Follies of 1910* unraveled quickly. Three days after the shooting, *The Denver Republican* reported that Joseph A. Murphy, von Phul's brother-in-law in St. Louis, was prepared to tell all. "We have no wish to drag anyone down, particularly a woman, but Mr. von Phul was not a barroom fighter, or a drunkard. We believe we can furnish information that will be invaluable and will ask that Henwood be held without bail until we can take the matter up with the Denver district attorney."

Even the *St. Louis Post-Dispatch* in von Phul's hometown jumped into the act, citing sources who claimed that a dinner party at the Brown Palace suite of Springer and his wandering spouse erupted into a scuffle between Henwood and von Phul in which a woman's voice, allegedly Mrs. Springer's, was heard to shout, "Don't kill him, Tony!"

Henwood's attorney denied all the speculation. "There is no ground for asserting that the quarrel between von Phul and Henwood was over a woman. When I say this, I speak advisedly. There was no woman with whom both men were infatuated, or in whom they were interested, or over whom they were jealous." He dropped a hint, however, that there was more to the case than what both men were saying. "We have no intention of drawing any woman into it. When von

Phul tore up Henwood's pictures…it was simply an act of malice. It was significant not in relation to any woman but merely as an expression of malice which von Phul might have shown in any other way." The next day, Henwood, speaking from his cell in the County Jail, warned that the papers "have done a great injustice by bringing my dearest friend into this matter. I think it is an outrage to bring that woman's name into the affair, when she had nothing to do with it."

Despite the denials, the papers avidly continued their pursuit linking Mrs. Springer to the incident. In the first days after the shooting she was "the woman in the case," "a Denver girl," or "a Denver society woman." By the time two days passed, she was named, and her photograph appeared in *The Post*. The lid was off. By June 5, *The Post* was convinced of the cause and printed the headline, "Von Phul Shot in Row Over Mrs. Springer, Friends Say." By this time, John Springer, ignorant of what had been going on between his wife and the St. Louis aeronaut, had seen and heard enough. He filed for divorce, based mainly on eight letters found in von Phul's hotel room, indicating, said *The Post,* "that Mrs. Springer enjoyed the most friendly relations with Von Phul."

Elliott's decision to try Henwood for the murder of Copeland was based not on protecting the reputations of the Springers, but on the relative merits of the case and on the likelihood of gaining a conviction. No matter which killing Henwood was tried for, von Phul and Mrs. Springer would be key figures. From the beginning, Bottom claimed that Henwood fired in mortal fear of his life and that self-defense would be the cornerstone of his case. Faced with a highly emotional scenario involving a prominent society couple and two headstrong gentlemen, the district attorney could not be sure that a jury wouldn't be sympathetic to Henwood's stance that he was only protecting his friend's marriage and convict him of manslaughter or even find him not guilty. Instead, Elliott invoked three sections of the Colorado Revised Statutes, 1908:

Section 1624—All murder which shall be perpetrated by means of poison etc. or perpetrated by any act greatly dangerous to the lives of others, and indicating a depraved mind, regardless of human life, shall be deemed murder in the first degree.

Section 1632—Justifiable homicide is the killing of a human being in necessary self-defense or in the defense of habitation, property or person against one who manifestly intends or endeavors by violence or surprise to commit a known felony, such as murder…upon either person or property or against any person or person, who manifestly intend and endeavor in a violent, riotous or tumultuous manner to enter the habitation of another for the purpose of assaulting or offering personal violence to any person, dwelling or being therein.

Section 1634—If a person kills another in self-defense it must appear that the danger was so urgent and pressing that, in order to save his own life or to prevent his receiving great bodily harm, the killing of the other must be absolutely necessary. And it must appear that the person killed was the assailant or that the slayer had really and in good faith endeavored to decline any further struggle before the mortal blow was given.

If von Phul fit the role of the aggressor in the barroom confrontation, Copeland, an uninvolved bystander, clearly did not. Henwood was to be tried for killing Copeland, whose name was barely mentioned, even though von Phul's name was called up frequently, and his relationship to Henwood explored repeatedly.

Bottom immediately called for a continuance, arguing that he was not prepared to fight the Copeland charge, that he was having trouble locating witnesses, that the district attorney's office would not let him look at Mrs. Springer's letters, that sensational newspaper coverage had prejudiced community opinion and, finally, that Mrs. Springer, the linchpin of the defense's arguments, was too ill to appear in court. Determined that the trial would proceed at a jaunty pace, Judge Whitford quickly dispensed with all the arguments and ruled that the trial would move ahead. One of the greatest legal battles in the history of criminal cases in Denver was launched.

Lawyer John Bottom's first order of business was to protest the method of selecting the jury. A recently passed ordinance had changed the jury system, one in which a group of "professional" jurors would sit for an entire term of the court, to a system in which the jury commissioner drew up a pool of names. Bottom, recognizing some of the potential jurors as "hanging jurors" from previous trials, said the jury should be selected under the new system. He was overruled.

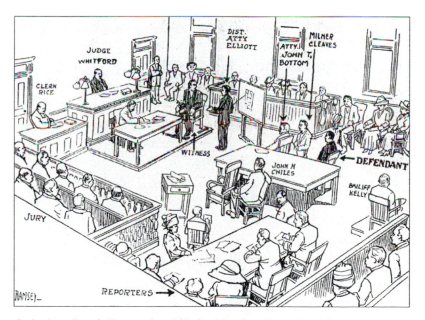

*Defendant Frank Henwood and his lawyers shared a table with the prosecution in the West Side Court during his 1911 trial. Reporters were allowed to sit next to the jury. (*Rocky Mountain News, *June 23, 1911. Courtesy of the Colorado Historical Society)*

Mrs. John W. Springer and her brother, Arthur Patterson. (The Denver Post, June 26, 1911. *Courtesy of the Colorado Historical Society)*

In anticipation of the appearance of the principals in the case, a large crowd waited patiently in the morning sun until the doors to the three-story court building were opened. Spectators rushed the courtroom and jostled for chairs. The losers had to be content with standing room along the walls. They had come to see Isabel Springer, who was expected to testify early in the trial. She did not appear, causing great disappointment. *The Post* reported, "Women with pompadours angrily jabbed them with nervous fingers; several girls forgot the amenities and measured the atmosphere with gum drawn through red lips; men shuffled their feet and a trio of daring youths started for the exit when reminded by the bailiff that those who were in could not get out, say, more than those who were out could not get in because Judge Whitford, jealous of his dignity and the order of the court, had ruled for locked doors."

If John and Isabel Springer, expected to have their first face-to-face meeting since he had filed for divorce, were no-shows, the star of the drama was front and center. Henwood, looking confident and walking erect and effortlessly, entered the courtroom and took his place next to Bottom. Women who had come to court to see if the prisoner was as attractive as some said were not let down. The reporter for *The Denver Times* noted,

> Henwood is fashioned after the model so conspicuously popular in the days when Reynolds, Rasburn and Lawrence painted belles and beaux. He is straight and lean, his shoulders are narrow, his head is small, having a slight sensual bulge at the base; his mouth, full-lipped and red, might belong to a stubborn, petulant girl who had known no other than her own way—a century ago he would have been a bravado of the road or court; today he is busy preparing to prove that he is not guilty of murder of Copeland since death came as the result of accident.

As he watched the selection of jurymen (women were not allowed to serve), Henwood's expression rarely changed. It became his habit to make notes in pencil on a pad and pass them to Bottom when he had a question or opinion. Except for the attorneys' brief squabble over how prospective jurors should be chosen, selection moved quickly. Bottom exercised all fifteen of his peremptory challenges before accepting the panel in its final form. On the jury were John Baxter, 67, solicitor; W. I. Bossler, 44, undertaker; James F. Buckley, 59, salesman; Albert Campbell, 41, locomotive engineer; M. Joseph Duval, 48, railroad man; Edward Erickson, 41, grocer; Bernard McCann, 30, clerk; John Reed, 70, real estate man; Martin Van Buren Sheldon, 71, retired railroad engineer; Charles E. Warren, 69, restaurant man; William L. Walker, 64, locomotive engineer; and William Wilshin, 64, bookkeeper. Nine of the twelve were married; Baxter had nine children.

Both sides outlined their cases in opening statements. Prominently displayed in one corner of the court, near the witness box, was a large drawing of the layout of the barroom. Prosecutor Elliott spoke first and took only four minutes to explain the state's case—that it was Henwood who pursued von Phul, purchased a gun, and shot the St. Louisan in the back, the last a charge the defense disputed. Defense attorney Bottom took his time to dispute newspaper accounts of what had happened on the night of May 24 and emphasized that Mrs. Springer had asked Henwood to retrieve the damaging letters with which von Phul threatened her. Henwood agreed to do it, argued Bottom, based on his friendship with Mr. Springer. He detailed, day by day, events leading up to the shooting.

❖

On June 23, the moment everyone had been waiting for arrived. Isabel Springer took the stand for the defense. Bottom hoped that she would bolster the defense's claims that Henwood fired out of fear for his safety by telling the jury about threats von Phul made toward Henwood. Bottom was convinced that the case would be won on her testimony.

Isabel was spirited from her room at the Savoy Hotel without the public knowing she would be testifying and was brought into court through the offices of the West Side Court building instead of through the usual courtroom entrance. She appeared at the witnesses' door to the courtroom without announcement, catching onlookers off guard. First to appear was her attorney, John T. Barnett, then her brother, Arthur Patterson, followed by Bottom and, finally, her personal physician, Dr. William Jayne, with Isabel supporting herself on his arm. She was said to be suffering from fatigue brought on by her fear of testifying and by the stress of her pending divorce.

She was attired in a demure blue serge suit with a wide white sailor collar, white gloves, and a wide-brimmed black straw hat covered with a veil of blue chiffon. Spectators couldn't help noticing the similarity of her outfit to the one worn by Evelyn Nesbit Thaw in the celebrated New York City trial that followed the shooting of architect Stanford

White in 1906. There were a remarkable number of parallels between the two cases, both of which involved wealthy, high-profile individuals, a beautiful woman, and two ardent pursuers, and a murder carried out in a public place in front of dozens of witnesses. Newspaper readers all over the country breathlessly followed the case in which the beautiful young Nesbit was seduced by White after an evening of champagne drinking. She later married a wealthy young Pittsburgh millionaire, Harry K. Thaw, "known for wide swings of personality, from kind and gentle to beastly cruel." After their marriage, he nagged Evelyn for the sordid details of her encounters with White and she spilled everything to him, causing him to go into a rage. On June 26, 1906, Thaw confronted White with a pistol at Madison Square Garden's rooftop theater and fired three times. Some thought the gunshots were part of the show until Evelyn shouted, "My God! He's shot him!"

Two sensational trials followed. The first, in 1907, ended in a hung jury and, after a second trial, Thaw was sent in February 1908 to an asylum for the criminally insane. In 1913, Thaw walked out of the asylum and fled to Canada. Two years later, another jury found him sane but declined to retry him because he had acted in a jealous rage. He continued to lead a dissolute life until his death in 1947 at the age of seventy-six. In an odd bit of historical convergence, Thaw visited Denver on a cross-country automobile vacation in 1915 and stayed in the bridal suite at the Brown Palace, where a large crowd waited almost two hours for him to emerge from the hotel's dining room.

If lovers of scandal were hypnotized by the Thaw case, they were no less so with the Brown Palace murder and with the beautiful Isabel Springer. They watched, fascinated, as she walked to the witness chair and sat with her hands nervously clutching her purse. Bottom began the questioning on which the trial, and Henwood's future, would turn. Mrs. Springer performed as either a clever avoider of direct responses or as a woman disoriented and under the influence of drugs. She had a difficult time understanding the questions and grew forgetful when it came time to respond.

Question: You may state your name, Mrs. Springer.

Answer: My name?

Q: Yes.

A: Isabel Springer.

Q: You are the wife of John W. Springer?

A: Yes, sir.

Q: Are you acquainted with Harold F. Henwood?

A: I am.

Q: Were you acquainted with Sylvester von Phul?

A: Yes, sir.

Q: On or about the 23rd day of May, did you know of a conversation had between Mr. Henwood and Mr. von Phul relating to the return of certain letters belonging to you?

At this point, prosecutor Elliott, not wanting testimony about Henwood's fear of von Phul to enter the record, began a series of interruptions. He found a willing accomplice in Judge Whitford.

Elliott: Objected to as incompetent, irrelevant and immaterial.

Court: Objection sustained.

Q: On the 24th day of May, which was the day, Mrs. Springer, preceding the night of the trouble in the barroom of the Brown Palace Hotel, did you have any conversation with Mr. von Phul relating to Mr. Henwood?

A: I don't understand your question.

Q: Did you have any conversation on that day?

A: On what day?

Q: The day of the night they had their trouble at the Brown Palace Hotel.

A: Did I what?

Q: Have any conversation with Mr. von Phul relating to Mr. Henwood?

A: May I have a minute, please? I cannot get your question clearly, Mr. Bottom.

MRS. JOHN W. SPRINGER ON THE WITNESS STAND

Spectators were quick to note that when Isabel Patterson Springer testified in the Henwood trial, her outfit was almost identical to that worn by Evelyn Nesbit in the sensational trial of Harry K. Thaw in New York City in 1907. (The Denver Post, *June 24, 1911. Courtesy of the Colorado Historical Society)*

Q: Did you have any conversation on the day of the shooting in the Brown Palace Hotel?

A: Did I have any conversation with...?

Q: With Mr. von Phul wherein Mr. von Phul spoke about Mr. Henwood?

A: Yes, sir.

Q: Did you ever have any conversation with Mr. von Phul after the dinner hour the evening before?

A: After dinner the evening before?

Q: Yes, immediately after you had had your dinner.

Here, even the attorneys became confused. Elliott couldn't follow the sequence of events and queried Bottom before both sides debated over the admissibility of Isabel's testimony. She sat silent on the stand while they argued.

Elliott: That is, on the twenty-third?

Bottom: Yes, in your apartment?

A: Did I have any conversation with him?

Q: With Mr. von Phul, yes, or did he have any with you?

Court: That is to be answered by yes or no.

A: Yes.

Q: You may state what occurred just as briefly as you can.

A: On that evening?

Q: On that evening.

Elliott vigorously blocked further questions about what the two had talked about, and when. Bottom again tried without success to introduce von Phul's threats against Henwood made to Isabel. Again, Elliott, with the judge's assistance, succeeded in preventing that from happening.

Finally, Bottom gave up and noted an exception (accepting the judge's ruling without agreeing to it): "Your honor. Now, may it please the court, as I understand the law, after an assault has been made by the deceased, testimony of the character that I am about to offer is proper to show the malice of the deceased toward the defendant in making the assault, and it is immaterial whether the assault is shown by the People in their main case or by the defendant in the defendant's case. Now, I understand that, your honor, to be the law.

Elliott: If your honor please, we have been over the law and there isn't any question about the law. We have been here since 9 o'clock and we have been examining one short witness that should have been examined in fifteen minutes.... It seems to me that this jury don't want to sit here until the Fourth of July.

Court: We are going to move.

After more wrangling with the judge over the admissibility of testimony, Bottom decided to bring Isabel's testimony to a close.

Bottom: If I understand the court now correctly, and I want to be advised, the court will not permit this witness to testify regarding any conversation had between her and Mr. von Phul wherein Mr. von Phul may have made threats toward Mr. Henwood, notwithstanding she may have communicated them to the defendant.

Court: In the present state of the record we will not receive the testimony.

Bottom: That is all, Mrs. Springer. You may stand aside for the present.

Isabel was helped from the witness stand by Dr. Jayne. She and Henwood, seated a few feet away, did not acknowledge each other. Her disoriented demeanor and testimony had done nothing to help the defendant.

❖

Elliott's legal maneuvering and the rulings of Judge Whitford left the defense attorney unable to enter Isabel Springer's testimony regarding threats von Phul may have made toward Henwood. Instead Bottom set about establishing a legal foundation on which to question Isabel: He called Henwood to the stand.

For his part, Henwood, with direction by his attorney, told his account of the events of May 23 and 24 that preceded the shooting. He emphasized that he was only trying to help a friend by getting Mrs. Springer's letters back from von Phul, and he told of his tussle with the St. Louisan in the latter's room at the Brown, in which a gun was pointed at him, and how he was so afraid that he took the precaution of purchasing a gun. He also made it clear that when he saw von Phul face-to-face in the hotel lobby on May 23, it was the first time they had met, contradicting pretrial rumors that the two men had fought over Isabel in St. Louis and in Denver.

Henwood insisted that he fired the fatal shots in self-defense. He told of his friendship with John Springer and his determination to protect his friend's marriage from ruin.

Bottom asked, "What conversation occurred between you and von Phul [at the bar]?"

Henwood answered, "I said, 'Tony, or Mr. von Phul,' because he objected to the name of Tony, 'won't you reconsider what you said this afternoon?' He said, 'I am going upstairs and get that gray-headed son of a bitch and pull him out of there and show him who is master here.' And I said, 'You can't get that over on me.'"

He told how von Phul knocked him down with one punch, then described the moment he emptied the gun at von Phul. "I got up and as I lifted myself there was only one thought in my mind, that was to see that man reach for a gun. I was almost certain that I did see him put his hand on his right hip. It was simply a movement on my part to protect myself and my life, and I pulled my pistol out and shot him." He insisted that von Phul was standing over him with "an expression of deadly hatred" when he fired the first shot.

As his testimony dragged on, Henwood began to lose control. Elliott's constant objections and Judge Whitford's sustaining them had the defendant so frustrated that he finally complained to the judge, "Let me ask you something. Am I not here to tell what happened? Why can't I tell? I only know one story." Judge Whitford reminded Henwood, and his attorneys, "The law prescribes a certain order of testimony in order to make the evidence that is introduced competent."

When Henwood came to the point in his testimony where he related pleading on bended knee with von Phul to release the letters and save Mr. Springer humiliation, he broke down in tears. His face went pale and he suddenly became unable to speak coherently. Plaintively, he turned to Judge Whitford and asked, "May I rest just a minute, your honor?" Judge Whitford replied, "Yes. Give him a glass of water." Henwood took two sips, then turned again to the judge. "May it please your honor to allow a recess. I am laboring under such a strain that I cannot go on." He told his attorney that he needed "to rest for a little while. I have sat in the court room so long this morning I have gotten dizzy." The court gave him an hour to compose himself.

Despite Henwood's insistence that he fired in self-defense, nearly every other witness didn't see it that way. A string of witnesses took the stand to testify that after he one-punched Henwood, von Phul turned back to the bar and placed his hands on the rail. The prosecution was quick to point out that, according to doctors, one bullet struck von Phul behind the right shoulder, although no one could say for certain which bullet it was.

Judge Whitford was speeding the trial along. By the fifth day, the prosecution had presented all its witnesses. Bottom incurred the judge's wrath when, caught by the haste with which the trial was progressing, he failed to have two of his witnesses in court. A sharp exchange between the two men unfolded before the jury.

"If we can't have testimony in this case, perhaps we can have books," chided Judge Whitford in reference to Bottom's attempts to read rules of testimony into the record. "I see you have some there."

"Yes, your honor. I would like to be heard upon that point. Can the jury be excused from the courtroom during the arguments?"

"No, Mr. Bottom. That is not necessary." Bottom made an exception, saying that the jurors should not hear discussions about the law. Moving on, he offered to read legal decisions about laying foundations for testimony. Judge Whitford cut him off.

"The law must be as it is, Mr. Bottom. Otherwise any man could kill any other man at any time without fear of the consequences." Before the judge finished speaking, Bottom was on his feet and said, "I take exception to the remarks of the court in the presence of the jury."

"And the court takes exception to the remarks of the attorney," the judge retorted.

"I must record my exception to the additional remarks of the court."

"The court is greatly displeased with the counsel for the defense in this case. You may proceed, Mr. Bottom, with the defense."

Clearly peeved when Bottom revealed that his witnesses were unavailable, Judge Whitford turned to the jury and said,

> We have endeavored to expedite matters, but it appears that the defense is unable to get its witnesses before this jury and, as the defendant has a right to be heard, the court can do nothing but order you confined and kept together. The court will instruct the bailiffs to permit you to go upon the lawn of the court house but you must remain together and must observe the order of the court in all respects and must permit none of your acquaintances or other persons to converse with you.

While he was in the business of chastising, Judge Whitford took a swipe at the newspaper coverage of the trial. "You must know, Mr. Jurors, that newspaper articles are not printed for the purpose of enforcing the law. They are conducted for other purposes to their own ends. It is not proper that you should read such comment on this case."

Having taken to task everyone who had annoyed him, Judge Whitford excused the jury and adjourned the trial until the following Monday.

Chapter Five

JOHN SPRINGER: "A BOOSTER, NOT A BOSS"

BORN ON JULY 16, 1859, in Jacksonville, Illinois, the son of attorney John T. Springer and a nephew of Congressman William M. Springer, John Wallace Springer discovered while a student at Asbury (now DePauw) University in Greencastle, Indiana, that he had extraordinary oratorical abilities, skills that would make him a popular speaker on patriotic holidays and would help him enormously in his political ambitions. He was an adept debater and was chosen to deliver the university's graduation speech in 1878.

After practicing law in Illinois for ten years, he moved to Texas where he married Eliza Clifton Hughes, the only daughter of wealthy Dallas banker and cattleman Col. William E. Hughes, on June 17, 1891. It was a marriage that would stand Springer in good stead, politically and financially. He took charge of Hughes's cattle interests, became a director of the Texas Cattle Raisers Association, and was involved in a number of other enterprises. The Springers had two daughters—Annie Clifton, born in 1892, and Sarah Elizabeth, who was born on November 10, 1898, and died nine months later. John and Eliza Springer, with daughter Annie, moved to Denver in 1896, hoping to improve Mrs. Springer's health. She had suffered with tuberculosis for years.

A year after their arrival in Denver, Springer became vice president of the Chamber of Commerce and two years later was named to the planning committee of the 1899 Festival of

Mountain and Plain, a weeklong Mardi Gras-style event that featured parades, masked balls, and general frivolity. It was begun by the business community in 1895 to destroy the "Silver Serpent" and chase away the economic depression brought on by the Crash of 1893, which followed repeal of the Silver Act that supported the federal government's purchase of huge amounts of silver. The repeal devastated Colorado's already shaky economy, heavily dependent on silver mining.

An avid breeder of horses, Springer convinced other members of the committee, including Wolfe Londoner, Otto P. Baur, John M. Kuykendall, David H. Moffat, and Charles Reynolds, that the festival needed to include a horse show and displays of Colorado's agricultural bounty. On Friday night of the festival "the finest horse show ever given in the West" took place under lights in the arena at Colfax and Broadway. The winners were given five thousand dollars in cash and premiums. It came off better than anyone dared hope. The horse show was one of the high points of the festival.

Springer was passionate about horses. With his father-in-law's financial backing, Springer bought up small ranches in an area south of Denver. Lenna May Cleveland, whose family homesteaded in the area, recalled in 1982, "Mr. Springer was a man of great wealth and fast action. In no time at all, he had bought up 12,000 acres of prairie grassland." His Cross Country Ranch became home to prize-winning Oldenburg horses, huge beauties popular in Germany as coach horses, that pulled his elaborate coach around town to the admiring gazes of the citizenry. Taken together, the rig and his four fine horses, each of which stood sixteen hands high, were estimated to be worth almost fifteen thousand dollars.

But his favorite was an animal imported from Germany. "He paid several thousand dollars for a beautiful animal he called The Colonel," remembered Cleveland, who, as a child visited the Springer spread frequently and saw the animal many times. "Colonel was Springer's pride and joy and he became a sort of a big pet at the ranch." In 1901, Springer ran afoul of a Colorado law that prohibited *docking*—cutting off the end of a horse's tail to keep it from becoming tangled in the harness. He was arrested, accused of bringing thirteen docked horses into the state, including the four that pulled his magnificent coach. The Humane Society declined to prosecute and turned the case over to the Denver District Court, but the charges were dropped.

Springer and his father-in-law, Colonel Hughes, were linked by marriage and also by their mutual love of show horses. In 1900 the two men figured prominently in the Denver Athletic Club show, a highlight of the society season that featured "plumes and flags and bunting [that] waved from the fence and the two long grandstands banking the arena. Society felt that the horse show was its very own, and society, in this particular, was not very far wrong." Entries belonging to Hughes and Springer won several ribbons, including classes for four-in-hand, turnouts, and saddle mares. Hughes was called "a great lover of coaching, the chase, dogs and horses and won many coaching prizes at horse shows."

Both men loved the finery and pomp of highly bred livestock, but both fell in love with the new plaything of the rich, the automobile. There were only 8,000 automobiles in the country at the turn of the century. Between 1900 and 1910, 460,000 of the new mode of transportation were sold, launching a national love affair that continues to this day. "Almost everyone was fascinated by the frail, costly, balky contraptions that, as one owner described them, 'shook and trembled and clattered, spat oil, fire, smoke and smell.'" The rich, who could most afford it first, began motoring the landscape in great numbers. In 1908, Colonel Hughes succumbed to the lure of the auto with his purchase of an eight-thousand-dollar, six-cylinder Pierce limousine. Springer, though he loved his horses and staged elaborate

*John W. Springer, circa
1911. (Courtesy of the
Denver Public Library,
Western History
Department)*

carriage parties at Overland Park racetrack for friends, also fell
hard for the motorized carriage, which was not without its per-
ils. In 1910, while driving back from the ranch with two passengers in his vehicle, Springer was involved in an accident with a
Tramway streetcar. He immediately assured all that he was not
going more than ten miles an hour and "we were on the right
side of the road with no thought of accident when suddenly the
Tramway car coming up from behind collided with us. It was
entirely the motorman's fault" [*The Post*, May 9, 1910].

His admiration of horses remained undiminished. In a
bylined article in *The Horse Show Monthly*, Springer predicted,

It is only day dreamers who venture to make the assertion
that the manufacture and use of the automobile will
eliminate entirely from America the horse in its various classes; such as these rush boldly into print and

announce that a Utopian age will arrive with the dawn of the twentieth century in which no horses will be seen on the streets, no saddle horses in the parks and no four-in-hand coaches in the mountains. This is all a wild vagary. It is the idlest talk to even intimate that the day of the horse has passed.

Beginning in 1901, he had built on a high point of the ranch property a baronial stone mansion, a castle, with turrets and a bright orange pennant with a large white S emblazoned on it. When it was completed, a large sign over the entrance proudly proclaimed: JOHN W. SPRINGER/CROSS COUNTRY CATTLE & RANCH/LITTLETON, COLORADO. It became a center of weekend entertainments for the state's political leaders. A man for whom connections were critical, Springer revealed years later that he kept a daily diary in which he noted the names of those who visited his spread.

He also found himself attracted to politics, where his oration abilities and outgoing personality were put to good use. In 1903, he gained fame for his Fourth of July speech at the Chautauqua auditorium in Boulder, Colorado. He was a powerful speaker. Even onetime newspaper reporter Polly Pry, who was not an admirer, said of Springer's speechmaking, "I never hear him speak without thinking of the Coney Island midway—what a 'barker' he would make! Well, we can't have everything—Coney's loss is Colorado's gain."

His Boulder speech began in the florid style of the day, "On the dial of the ages liberty cast its first shadow across the pathway of despots with the American Declaration of Independence…" and went on for two hours. His speech attracted the attention of those in the Republican Party, and they began to take notice of his effect on crowds. He was a devout civic booster and much in demand as an after-dinner speaker, which helped launch his political career.

❖

The high-water mark of Springer's political ambitions was the Denver mayoral election of 1904. The state's Republican Party was badly split between supporters of Senator Edward O. Wolcott and those who opposed him. A tumultuous convention held in April 1904 at Denver's Coliseum to select the party's candidate for mayor concluded with unanimous support for Springer. Beaming before the cheering throng that filled the hall, the nominee, wearing a long-tailed Prince Albert coat, mounted the speaker's platform. "Springer for mayor!" yelled a supporter from the back of the hall. The crowd seconded the emotion. The chairman rapped his gavel for order as Professor Sigel's band pounded out a patriotic tune, "Uncle Sammy."

Finally the crowd fell silent. Springer spoke. "Now the band will give us 'A Hot Time in the Old Town' and then we'll be ready for it." The delegates roared with laughter as the band played. After paying tribute to the party's leaders, President Theodore Roosevelt and Governor James H. Peabody, Springer launched into his first, impassioned campaign speech:

> The great, united Republican party is once again alive to its duty and its magnificent opportunity. It stands for decency in politics and for the maintenance of the standards of good citizenship and, I want to say, that, if you have never been in a fight before, you are going to see one during the next thirty days. You will see meetings at the crossroads of the honest and liberty-loving citizens of all classes and they will demonstrate that they and only such as they will run this town during the next four years.

Denver politics were a corruptive pit at the dawn of the twentieth century. The 1904 campaign was one of the nastiest and most crooked in the city's history. George Creel, a former newspaper reporter, observed in *Rebel at Large*, "The tramway company, the water company, the telephone company, the coal companies, the smelters—all operating as a unit—controlled both parties and named both tickets in every election. The Supreme Court, members of the legislature, mayors, county officials, and councils were 'hired hands,' taking their orders from the Big Mitt." Muckraking writer David Graham Phillips, writing about a similar situation in the U.S. Senate, called them "the unblushing corruptionists."

Springer ran as a progressive Republican, determined to reform the city's corrupt political system that allowed "the combine," providers of the city's public utilities, to determine

John Springer renamed the home on his twelve-thousand-acre Cross Country Ranch "Castle Isabel" after his marriage to Isabel Patterson Folck in 1907. Frank Henwood was a frequent guest. (Courtesy of the Littleton Historical Museum)

who would sit in the mayor's office. In accepting his party's nomination, Springer told the gathered officials, "From this city the wires will tell on election night that Denver has repudiated the election outrages that has debauched her in the past. The record of corruption of Democratic officials will eternally damn that party."

His opponent, Robert W. Speer, was backed by the vast financial and political support of the utilities, especially from William G. Evans and the Denver Tramway Company, who were determined to orchestrate the outcome of the 1904 election. An ardent Republican, Evans nevertheless backed Speer, a Democrat, to maintain the status quo that allowed the utilities to reap huge financial returns with little regulation from the city.

The mayoral election drew five candidates—John Hipp, Prohibitionist; J. W. Martin, Socialist; George E. Randolph, Anti-Wolcott Republican; John W. Springer, Civic-Republican; and Robert W. Speer, Democrat. Only Springer and Speer were serious contenders, and some observers dismissed Springer as little more than a sacrificial lamb for the Evans machine. But Springer ran a spirited campaign. In a fiery speech before the Young Men's Republican Club, he launched a blistering attack on "ballot box stuffers," "thugs," and "the machine." He recounted how a friend had been knocked down at a polling place during a previous election while a policeman watched passively. "Had a Democratic policeman laid his hand on me there would have been more dead Democrats at that polling place than could have been conveniently buried in one day." The crowd "hurrahed for several minutes…while the speaker stood and smiled and beamed upon his audience."

Springer had the avid support of *The Denver Post*, which vigorously opposed Speer and his corporate backers during the campaign but, after his election, supported Speer just as vigorously. The day before the election, *The Post* editorialized on the differences between the two candidates. "Mr. Speer's character is well known. As [a] member of the board of fire and police he put political rustlers on the police and detective force. He has been responsible for the doings of the election commission because he could have stopped the game, in which they were puppets, with a word. The shameless padding of the registration would not have gone on had he set himself against it."

On the other hand, *The Post* regarded Springer as "a booster, not a boss. Mr. Springer is young [he was 45 at the time], energetic and ambitious." The paper almost daily ran an anti-Speer cartoon on page one, including one in which Speer, dressed as a knight and carrying a shield that read "I Do Things for the Corporations," timidly enters a spooky forest where every tree has Springer's face staring sternly at him.

When the votes were counted, Springer was defeated 29,544 to 24,565, a difference of 4,979 votes, most of which came in the poorer precincts where voter fraud was practiced openly. Speer, a consummate political manipulator, and his administration provided a kind of early-day welfare program in which policemen gave coupons to the poor, who could redeem them at local saloons for sandwiches and beer, assuring that both voters and saloonkeepers, a powerful political force, would remember his largesse at elections.

Particularly blatant was the use of repeaters, operatives who voted under several names in a single precinct. In the Third Ward, two men, each representing himself as Robert Ihle, voted within ten minutes of each other. James Warren, dead for six years, nevertheless exercised his civic duty. One young man showed up at the polls with three voter cards. When asked his name, he said, "Either Love, Lawton or Long. I don't care which," and voted. In the poorer, traditionally Democrat wards, Speer ran up overwhelming numbers—3,182 to 741 in the Fourth Ward, for example—which Springer was unable to overcome in other parts of the city. Speer backer Walter S. Cheesman commented after the election, "It cost us more to defeat Springer than any other man who ever ran for office in Denver!"

On May 22, 1904, only five days after his election loss, Springer's thirty-five-year-old wife, Eliza, finally lost her struggle with tuberculosis and died at the couple's home at 930 Washington Street, leaving him a single parent of their eleven-year-old daughter, Annie. Eliza's declining health had been a constant concern for him throughout the campaign and, commented in the *News*, "her husband's campaign is believed to have sustained the waning strength of the invalid." Tragedy would strike again at the Washington Street mansion when his seventy-two-year-old mother, Sarah, fell down a small flight of stairs and died on January 10, 1909.

After the results of the mayoral election were made public, there was talk of a protest but Springer decided against it. First, contesting the election would cost fifteen thousand dollars, with no guarantee that the fraud would be rooted out. But there was another reason, one not revealed until the

John Springer's political ambitions knew few bounds. In 1904, he went to the Republican convention in Chicago believing he would be selected as vice presidential running mate for President Theodore Roosevelt. He wasn't. (Dick Kreck collection)

following September during the state convention of the Republican Party at the Broadway Theater. Still a force in Republican politics, a smoldering Springer rose at the convention to nominate his good friend, Greeley W. Whitford, for congressman-at-large. While he was at it, the vanquished mayoral candidate took the opportunity to excoriate the election process, and the men behind it:

> I will tell you, my friends, why our contest for the municipal election has not been prosecuted. Mr. Will Evans came to the office of my trust company, where I and several of my fellow candidates on the Republican city ticket were assembled and he said to us there, 'Mr. Springer and gentlemen, unless you desist from this contest you will have the four public utility corporations of this city buck you and your trust company at every point.' What could we do? It was annihilation for us to proceed, and we laid down. But I tell you, fellow Republicans, over in the court-house, locked up from the vision of honest men, are the ballots of the last election, which tell of the election of the entire Republican city ticket by majorities ranging from 6,000 to 7,000 votes. And those ballot boxes are sealed by the word and will of the man who keeps Bob Speer and his cohorts in office today.

Springer further explained to the delegates why he decided not to contest the election. "I conferred with others interested in pushing the cases and said, 'Boys, we had better quit before we begin. We have not money enough to beat four corporations in this town.'" Evans denied all the charges.

Springer had a word, too, for those Republicans who heeded the call of the manipulators behind the Speer campaign and voted Democratic. "There are people upon this platform who fought the Republican ticket in every ward. There were thousands of good and loyal Republicans who gave their time, work and money to elect the Republican ticket who are not in this convention, but many of you who are today claiming the right to dictate the nominations of this convention did not support that ticket at all. All that I ask of them now is that they will not go out from this convention after nominating this ticket and secretly knife it as they did before."

The cheering crowd egged him on with cries of "Give it to 'em!" and "You're right, John!" He kept up his diatribe until one delegate shouted, "Why don't you nominate yourself?"

John Springer's show horses and fine carriages were the envy of Denver's equestrian set, and he frequently entertained guests for horse shows at the city's Overland Park. (Denver Newsletter & Colorado Advertiser, June 20, 1908. Courtesy of the Colorado Historical Society)

Springer turned toward the catcaller and said sternly, "Let me tell whoever made that insulting remark that if he and his kind had been in with the Republicans on the 17th day of May, I should have been mayor of Denver this moment!"

Springer's political career, which began with him as a Democrat until he went to work for the William McKinley presidential campaign in 1896, never again reached such heights. In the fall of 1904, he was strongly supported by Western cattle interests to run as vice president on the Republican ticket with President Theodore Roosevelt. He went to the national convention in Chicago with high hopes but returned empty-handed. The same year, his name was mentioned, briefly, in the Colorado gubernatorial race but his excoriation of Republican defectors to the cause of Speer and the Democrats in 1904 did not earn him the love of the loyalist element of the party. Political commentator Polly Pry, in her magazine of the same name, observed,

> Hereafter precautions should be taken to prevent this erratic political adventurer from getting inside the doors of a Republican convention hall. By his action…at the state convention, he forfeited all right to claim association with Republicans as a member of the party, and not only did he read himself out of the party…but he read himself out of the confidence and trust of everyone connected with the organization and of gentlemen generally. When John W. Springer made that harangue, attacking the party and party leaders, he was acting as the mouthpiece of a few bandits who, disgruntled at their loss of influence and prestige in the party, are banded together to work to the defeat of the ticket this fall.

His political ambitions blunted, he was still an important figure in the state Republican Party when President

Roosevelt visited Denver in May 1905. An elaborate banquet was staged for the president on the top floor of the Brown Palace Hotel with many of the city's leading businessmen in attendance, including Walter Cheesman, Edward P. Costigan, Charles Kountze, Edward Keating, Wolfe Londoner, John Shafroth, George Tritch, and Edwin Van Cise. Springer was seated at one of the head tables, along with former governor James Peabody, Dennis Sheedy, and Crawford Hill. Speakers, including Mayor Speer, a Democrat, rose one after the other to praise Roosevelt and his programs. Springer was not called upon.

In 1906, he was touted as a possible U.S. Senate candidate, but when the fractured Republican Party gathered in Denver that fall, it was Simon Guggenheim, backed by the political machine, who got the party's Senate nomination. Springer often inserted his name into the discussions whenever a high political office came available. Newspaper editors took note. In July 1906, the *Ouray Plain Dealer* editorialized, "Springer is going up like a rocket just now, or thinks he is, but he will come down like a stick this fall. Springer takes himself very seriously. He thought he was going to run for the vice presidency with Roosevelt, but he ran for mayor instead, and did not run very fast either." He was dismissed by the *Leadville Courier* as "another four-foot boat with a six-foot whistle." Polly Pry sniped, "Few people seem to take John W. Springer seriously. There's nothing serious about a joke." The abortive Senate campaign was his last attempt at political office.

❖

In April 1907, Springer, forty-seven, married Isabel Patterson Folck, a twenty-seven-year-old St. Louis divorcée with a reputation as a carefree socialite whom he had courted in St. Louis and Denver the previous summer.

Springer ensconced his bride in the red brick, seven-bedroom mansion at 930 Washington Street, built in 1891 by Edwin B. Hendrie, president of Hendrie & Bolthoff, a Denver manufacturer of mining equipment. Springer paid nineteen thousand dollars for the house in September 1903. Almost immediately, he added two lots to the property and built a large carriage house for his prized horses. Irene Frye Gay, whose family bought the house in 1926 when she was ten years old, heard "the old lady across the alley" tell her mother numerous tales about Isabel. "She used to come out in the thinnest of negligees and stand on the stoop and give orders to the servants. She was not a principled, devoted wife."

Springer's wealthy ex-father-in-law, Colonel Hughes, did not approve of Springer's courtship of Isabel because she had been married and divorced and because she was known in St. Louis as a free spirit seen frequently at balls and other amusements. He had checked. Hughes convinced a judge of Isabel's unsavory reputation, and he was appointed guardian of Springer's fourteen-year-old daughter, Annie Clifton Springer, after her mother's death, and moved with her to St. Louis in January 1907. She called her grandparents Gramps and Bammy. Two years later, Hughes severed his connection with Springer and with the Continental Trust Company by selling the firm's assets to a syndicate headed and organized by his former son-in-law. The transaction included the Continental Building at Sixteenth and Lawrence Streets in Denver, and Springer succeeded Hughes as president of the company.

Annie, a tall, red-haired beauty known as Clifton to her friends to differentiate her from her grandmother, also named Annie, returned to Denver in 1912 and married Lafayette Hughes, son of the late Senator Charles J. Hughes (no relation to Colonel Hughes). Her grandfather moved to remain close to her. Worth an estimated ten million dollars, the colonel built an elaborate home for the newly wed Hugheses and a thirty-six-room mansion for himself on an entire block of land in Denver's exclusive Country Club

*Janette Lotave
Springer, John W.
Springer's third wife.
(*Rocky Mountain
News, *August 25,
1915. Courtesy of
the Colorado
Historical Society)*

neighborhood. At the same time, he reacquired the bulk of the stock in the Continental Trust Company, buying two thousand shares of Springer's three thousand shares in the firm.

Springer divorced Isabel in 1911, following the scandal at the Brown Palace, and in 1915, now fifty-six years old, he married for a third time. Again, his bride was a much younger woman, Janette Elizabeth Orr Muir Lotave, who, like Isabel before her, was twenty-seven years old when she went to the altar with Springer. Asked how she and her new husband met, Janette replied smartly, "I have known Mr. Springer for the last ten years. He was a very dear friend of our family. We decided that we should get married, and that is all there is to it." Springer, who bought and sold Denver properties with alacrity and owned fine homes in various parts of the city, moved his bride into the newly purchased and newly christened Springer Lodge, formerly the five-acre country estate of J. J. Henry, at 1655 Vrain Street, with 125 feet of frontage on Sloan Lake.

Janette guarded her age closely. It doesn't appear on the couple's marriage certificate, on her death certificate, or on her cemetery headstone, but, according to information given in the U.S. Census, she was thirty-two years old in 1920. She, too, was a divorcée, whose marriage at seventeen to Parisian painter Carl Lotave had ended in Colorado Springs in 1909. Springer and his bride, equally as beautiful as Isabel, were married on August 26, 1915, in a private ceremony at the El Tovar Apartments, 1515 Grant Street, with her sisters, Josephine Aymer and Katharine Muir, as witnesses. Neither the bride nor the groom had attendants.

Springer made every effort to erase his four-year marriage to Isabel. On the couple's marriage license he listed his previous wife as deceased and answered "No" on the line marked "Divorced?" In *Who Was Who in America*, the new Mrs. Springer is listed as his second wife, ignoring the existence of Isabel. Information on file in the alumni office of DePauw University, his alma mater, makes no mention that Janette was his third wife.

❖

One more great public appearance on a grand stage remained. Springer's oratorical abilities led him to be called upon to deliver the eulogy for the Elks Club at the elaborate funeral for William F. "Buffalo Bill" Cody in Denver on January 14, 1917. The Great Scout's farewell was a majestic affair befitting the man whose frontier exploits made him the idol of millions. His body lay in state in the rotunda of the state capitol, where eighteen thousand admirers passed by his open casket in three hours. An estimated ten thousand people were waiting in below-freezing temperatures in a line that snaked from the capitol's Colfax Avenue entrance up Broadway to Sixteenth Street when the coffin was closed and the funeral procession moved slowly to the Elks Lodge at Fourteenth and California Streets. Governors, legislators, Civil War veterans, aging cowboys, wizened mountain men, and dignitaries in a long line of automobiles were among those who bade him farewell.

Springer, a member of the Elks Denver Lodge No. 17, was in full flower when he intoned the praises of Cody, a friend and fellow Elk. He was at his oratorical best:

> With his upturned face to the noonday sun, William Frederick Cody, on January 10th, 1917, met the death angel face to face, and drifted out into a dreamless sleep that knows no waking. It was the peaceful ending of the most picturesque life in American history. As his friend I lay my humble tribute this Sabbath afternoon in the lodge room of the Elks' Home of Denver, Colorado, upon the bier of him whose achievements are the household knowledge of the entire world.

With America's entry into World War I less than three months away, Springer took the opportunity to link patriotism and Cody, "who blazed the way for his generation, who subdued the wild beasts, fought the Indians, bridged the rivers, tunneled the mountains, built the railways and made an empire out of a wilderness which is now inhabited by millions of prosperous, happy and contented Americans."

He added,

> God forgive the misdirected and misguided Americans who in their mad scramble for wealth, are neglecting, opposing and maligning efforts now being made to defend this matchless heritage bequeathed to us. We owe unswerving allegiance to the army and navy of the United States, and we should prepare for the future a complete and adequate defense. We should compel military training as the surest preventative of war.

He concluded on a stirring note:

> Sleep on, Old Scout! Under the aegis of the old flag, our hallowed Stars and Stripes, may he rest forever and a day. His grave shall catch the first light of the rising sun, while the moon and ten thousand stars keep watch when the shadows have dropped down from the eternal snowcapped peaks beyond. The mountain pines shall sing their requiems about his tomb, and in the hush and peacefulness of this abode, the spirit of William Frederick Cody shall live and dwell with us like a sweet benediction, forever and forever.

After the scandal of 1911, Springer withdrew slowly from public life. He began to sell off pieces of his Cross Country Ranch and to spend more of his time in town. In 1913, he sold the remaining property to Colonel Hughes, who died in 1918 and left the ranch to his granddaughter—Springer's daughter—Annie.

In 1932 Springer, then seventy-three years old, underwent surgery to remove a cancerous tumor in his abdomen. Though he survived, he never fully recovered his health. His life was darkened again by tragedy in 1940, when Annie committed suicide in the bathroom of her Country Club mansion with a single .32-caliber bullet to her heart. Annie, forty-eight years old, was suffering from an ear ailment but believed she had a malignant growth in her head. An autopsy revealed that her fears were unfounded. Annie's will provided evidence of how far her father's fortunes had waned. Among the state's wealthiest women, Annie specified that her father be allowed to live in her home and that he receive twenty-five hundred dollars annually from her estate as long as he lived.

His time as a power broker long past and in poor health, Springer chose to live quietly in a small house in Littleton until his death at age eighty-five on January 10, 1945. He was the last living principal in one of the most sensational scandals in Denver history. His wife Janette died in 1957, and they are buried beside each other in Littleton Cemetery under a huge blue spruce and a simple granite marker that reads: SPRINGER/JANETTE E./DIED OCT. 3, 1957/JOHN W./1859-1945.

Chapter Six
GUILTY: "A PROSECUTING JUDGE"

MONDAY, JUNE 26, 1911, another day in which the thermometer was predicted to reach 90, promising another stifling courtroom, began with a surprise. Prosecutor Willis V. Elliott, who battled ferociously for more than a week to keep out of the proceedings testimony that Tony von Phul had threatened Frank Henwood, had a change of heart.

When the trial resumed, thirty minutes late, Elliott rose and addressed the court:

> If your honor pleases, there has been a good deal of discussion here between court and counsel with reference to the admission of threats. The state has uniformly objected to these admissions. I think there is no question about the law, never was any question about it. I want to say to counsel now, that if they have such testimony as that, so far as objection on the part of the state is concerned, it will not be made and they may introduce all of it without objection. We want it understood now, as we say, we don't want any technicality to prevent the introduction of any testimony the defendant is entitled to. We don't want any conviction upon that.

Defense attorney John Bottom disagreed with Elliott's interpretation of the law on self-defense, but he was delighted to seize the opportunity to bring into the record what led Henwood to believe his life was in danger. A successful plea of self-defense was his only hope. Some legal experts believed that the prosecutor's reversal would open the floodgates of testimony and make public the most salacious of exhibits—Isabel Springer's heated love letters to von Phul. It was a risk Elliott was willing to take because of the law that ruled that the accidental killing of a bystander—in this case George Copeland—is murder. Though von Phul was the focus of testimony, Henwood was on trial for killing Copeland.

As the day's first witness, a well-rested Henwood resumed his careful narrative, recounting, almost minute-by-minute, events leading to the showdown in the barroom of the hotel. He told how von Phul grabbed Isabel's arm at the Orpheum Theater and how a distraught Isabel told him that von Phul came to her apartments, struck her, and tore up two photographs of Henwood.

Henwood told the court that Isabel warned him, "'You don't know what kind of man you're dealing with'; that he was absolutely desperate and would go to any length. I still thought I could appeal to the best side of him." Cross-examined closely by Elliott, Henwood was alternately evasive, engaging, nervous, and confident. Elliott contended that Henwood acted, not out of concern for his friend John Springer, but out of jealousy over von Phul's attentions to Isabel.

Elliott grilled Henwood on his visits to police Chief Hamilton Armstrong, whom Henwood had asked to intervene. Henwood fudged his testimony.

Question: Didn't you ask the chief to run von Phul out of town? Didn't you say, "He is annoying her, Mrs. Springer, and I want the son of a bitch run out of town?"

Answer: No.

Q: Didn't you tell the chief this: "If he," meaning von Phul, "sends those letters to Springer, I'll beat John to it—I'll kill the bastard myself"?

A: Not that way, Mr. Elliott. I simply pointed . . .

Q: I don't care what you pointed. I want to know if you said that.

A: I said, "John Springer is a big man here in Denver and if this man carries out his threat, John will kill him. This would ruin him. Rather than have this come about I had almost rather do it myself."

It was, Henwood said, after he received a note from Isabel, urging him to stay away from her, that he went to a hardware store on Lawrence Street and purchased the first gun he ever owned. The legal groundwork about threats laid, Bottom called for the woman in the case to return to testify. She was still in her rooms at the Savoy Hotel, but a phone call and a twenty-minute delay found her back on the stand.

It was a far more composed Isabel Springer. She wore a plain tailored suit highlighted by a black velvet bow at the neck. As she had three days earlier, she wore a hat draped with a veil of blue chiffon. Her voice was clear ("a cooing soprano of softest, pleasing quality, steady as the unstruck string of a piano," gushed *The Denver Times*) and her small hands, clad in white gloves, remained at rest in her lap. Her feet were planted firmly on the witness stand.

Bottom immediately set about having her recite threats she heard von Phul make against Henwood. He pinpointed a note she had delivered to Henwood by her maid on the morning before the shooting. "You may state to the jury as near as you can the contents of that communication."

"I don't remember the exact contents, Mr. Bottom, excepting that I said that I thought it was best for him not to come to our apartment anymore, for I thought it would be dangerous for him to do so."

Bottom wanted more. "What, if anything, did you communicate to Mr. Henwood either in this communication or through the mail with reference to Mr. von Phul having told you with reference to his getting a room on the sixth floor of the Brown?"

"He said he had gotten a room [603] right next to the elevator, and that if he saw Mr. Henwood going to my apartment with Mr. Springer or alone that he would immediately come in and 'fix him'; that was his expression."

Early on, her testimony strengthened the defense's case that the promoter acted out of fear of von Phul and with justification when he opened fire in the barroom. But, then, Bottom committed the unpardonable lawyering sin—he asked one question too many.

Question: When did you communicate to Mr. Henwood the fact that Mr. von Phul struck you on the evening as you have related?

Answer: Why, I think it was the following morning, Mr. Bottom.

Q: Now, will you state what you said to Mr. Henwood, as near as you can remember?

A: I just stated that I begged him that he let me alone and let me take care of myself.

Bottom quickly tried to turn her testimony to other subjects but it was too late. The question was planted in jurors' minds: If she asked Henwood to withdraw, why did he continue to pursue von Phul? His defense that he was only acting to save his friend's marriage was dealt a mortal blow.

Later in her testimony, Isabel denied that she had told Frank Loveland, Henwood's close friend, that she had felt a gun in von Phul's pocket when she, her mother, and von Phul took a drive to the ranch on the morning of the shooting. "I will ask you if you do not remember telling Frank Loveland on that day and after that ride, that you felt a gun in Mr. von Phul's pocket?" Bottom pressed. "I did not," Isabel answered, emphatically.

Both attorneys handled Mrs. Springer with gloves as soft and white as her own. Bottom barely challenged her claims that she pleaded with Henwood to let her deal with von Phul. On cross-examination, Elliott questioned her politely, showing none of the dogged aggressiveness that he displayed when

*Crowds lined up to watch John T. Bottom, left, and Frank Henwood walk from the courthouse to the jail. (*Rocky Mountain News, *June 24, 1911. Courtesy of the Colorado Historical Society)*

questioning Henwood. He did, however, keep returning to whether she had asked Henwood to withdraw from her affairs.

Question: Did you ask Mr. Henwood to assist you in any way?

Answer: Yes, I asked him to help me, but later begged him to drop the whole affair and leave me to handle it.

Q: Were you pleased with Mr. Henwood's manner of handling this situation?

A: I was not.

Q: What did you say to him?

A: I told him he was handling it wrong and for him to let it alone and allow me to treat it in my own way.

Q: And told him you wanted him to keep out?

A: I asked him not to do it.

Q: You pleaded with him and begged that he let it alone?

A: Yes, sir.

Q: You told him he was making a mistake?

A: Yes, sir.

Q: Said to keep out of it; the only way to avoid trouble is for you to keep out of it, didn't you?

A: To let me do it myself.

Q: And the only way to avoid trouble was to keep out of it?

A: I feared there would be trouble if he did not stop right where he was.

Inexplicably, her letters, the ones that precipitated the whole incident, were never brought up, never introduced into evidence. Except for portions of those that appeared in the newspapers, their contents were never revealed. When she was excused, all agreed that Mrs. Springer had been a splendid witness for herself, protecting her reputation at the expense of the man to whom she had gone for help. In her mind, Henwood and von Phul were little more than acquaintances, one of whom she knew casually in St. Louis and the other whom she knew as a business associate of her husband. Although a witness for the defense, she did much to bolster the prosecution's case.

❖

On Tuesday, June 27, the sensational tales that spectators who packed the sweltering courtroom had been waiting to hear finally surfaced. Determined to prove that Henwood's motives for the shooting went far beyond his friendship with John Springer, Elliott asked Henwood about an incident at the Cross Country Ranch a week before the showdown at the Brown Palace. On Wednesday, May 17, as they had done many times, Henwood, Mrs. Springer, and her maid, Irma Braasch, went from the Brown Palace to the ranch, driven there by Thomas Lepper, the family chauffeur for sixteen years. It was a busy three days before John Springer arrived on Saturday afternoon, according to the testimony of Cora Carpenter, the Springers' housekeeper at the ranch since early March. She told the rapt courtroom how she had unexpectedly come across Henwood and Mrs. Springer in the ballroom of the house. "Mr. Henwood was seated in a chair and Mrs. Springer stood in front of him. Mr. Henwood had his arms around Mrs. Springer's hips and she had her hands on his shoulders." When they saw her, she said, "Mrs. Springer pushed Henwood's shoulders back and Henwood released her."

There was more. She related that Henwood spent his first night at the ranch in a bed in John Springer's office on the first floor of the castle. The second night, she said, Henwood and Lepper moved the bed upstairs to the Red Room, connected to Mrs. Springer's bedroom by a shared bathroom. Carpenter recounted that Henwood went to Mrs. Springer's room about 5 P.M. to see if she were all right after she had taken a spill from her horse earlier in the afternoon. She didn't see him come out. She did, however, see the maid carry trays of whiskey up to the room several times during the night.

The next morning, she said, she found Mrs. Springer's nightgown "torn into strips in front and about the neck." Elliott then asked what condition Mrs. Springer's bed was in.

Mrs. Cora Carpenter. (The Denver Post, *June 14, 1913. Courtesy of the Colorado Historical Society)*

"It was rumpled and in great disorder."

"Had it been slept in?"

"It had been occupied." And, she noted, Henwood's bed had remained unoccupied all night.

Henwood's attorney was not about to let her testimony pass unchallenged. Irma Braasch, the maid, had left town and could not be found to testify, but Bottom tried to discredit Cora Carpenter's testimony.

Question: You say the maid carried liquor to the room while Mrs. Springer and Henwood were there?

Answer: Yes.

Q: One glass?

A: One glass the first time, but two glasses the second time.

Q: And how many trips did she make?

A: I don't know. Eight or ten during the evening.

Q: What did they do with the liquor?

A: I don't know. Drank it, I suppose.

Q: As a matter of fact, you do not know what was done with the liquor, do you?

A: I know it was consumed.

Q: Do you? Mrs. Springer might have shampooed her hair with it for all you know to the contrary, mightn't she?

A: I know it was consumed. She might have watered the palms with it.

Q: Did she have any palms around her room?

A: No, sir.

Q: Then what do you mean by your remark?

A: Well, I heard that one time she did water her palms with whiskey.

Q: Where?

A: At the Brown Palace Hotel.

Laughter erupted among the spectators. Judge Whitford was not amused. "At the next manifestation of levity during this trial the bailiffs shall open the doors and clear the court-room. This is not a theater."

During his turn in the witness chair, Henwood, perspiring heavily in the humid closeness of the room, denied any impropriety. Despite close questioning by Elliott, he refuted Carpenter's testimony that she had surprised him and Isabel Springer in a compromising embrace and added, cryptically, "I wouldn't have cared if she did see me." He maintained that he spent only a few minutes in Isabel's room and that he did not drink while he was there.

❖

With no more witnesses to be heard, Judge Whitford began the morning session of June 28 by taking thirty-five minutes to instruct the jury on the options for their verdict. He told the jurors that if they did not believe that Henwood was justified in shooting von Phul, they must find him guilty of murder in either the first or second degree. "There is no manslaughter in this case."

He laboriously explained the law:

> If you find from the evidence that the defendant, Henwood, at the time he fired the shot or shots at the said von Phul, honestly and in good faith believed his life was in danger, or that he was in danger of suffering great bodily harm, although such danger was not real, but apparent; and if the circumstances induced in him a reasonable belief that he was in actual danger of losing his life, or suffering great bodily harm, and if he acted from real and honest conviction as to the character of the danger induced by reasonable evidence, and not in a spirit of revenge or jealousy; he fired the said shots at the said von Phul in his necessary self-defense, and that by mistake the shots struck the deceased George E. Copeland, from the effects of which he died, then you are instructed to find the defendant not guilty.

He went on to define what circumstances constituted first- or second-degree murder. While the judge read his instructions, Henwood sat passively, staring at him without expression. Bottom immediately launched into a long list of exceptions, including that the court failed to explain the circumstances of the shooting, that he drew too rigid a definition of self-defense and, most important, that Judge Whitford did not give the jury the option of finding Henwood guilty of manslaughter. There were thirteen exceptions in all.

Day turned to night, but the trial went on. Determined to wrap up the case before another day passed, Judge Whitford called for a night session. Despite this, the courtroom was stifling and open windows allowed only slight breezes to enter. The temperature in Denver had risen to 94 degrees earlier in the day. *The Times* described the air as "foul, dank and laden with that undefinable odor found only where many are crowded together, perspiring and uncomfortable."

After Bottom read his exceptions into the record, Deputy District Attorney John Chiles began his portion of the prosecution's summation. He restated the judge's instructions and urged the jury to bring back a verdict of first-degree murder. "The charge here is for shooting and killing George E. Copeland, not von Phul. Henwood has the right to be tried for the Copeland shooting and, if convicted, then punished for that act. His actions and intentions towards von Phul are the measure of his liability in the murder of Copeland."

Chiles told the jury not to be fooled by Henwood's claim that he was trying to save the Springers' marriage.

> He told you that in endeavoring to protect the name of his beloved friend, John Springer, he shot von Phul, that he was trying to protect John Springer's family. In this affair, he was trying also to protect the name of that fair creature—the wife of his friend, Mr. Springer....

Do you believe he was telling the truth? If you do, you are easy, gentlemen of the jury, and I know you want to be fair. We showed you, gentlemen of the jury, a condition of affairs which amounts to this: Taken into the bosom of Springer's family and received with open arms, Henwood took advantage of that fact—that kind and courteous treatment—and he destroyed Springer's home. And then he tells you he was acting in Springer's interest, after he had wrecked his home on the shores of lust and damnable, treacherous desire. Great God, is there no justice for a man like that?

I'll tell you what Henwood was acting under. He had had illicit relations with Mrs. Springer and he knew it, and he feared that von Phul stood higher in the affections of this lady than he did.

For a mind-numbing six hours, relieved only by a break for dinner, Bottom once again walked the jury through the events leading up to the shooting and emphasized Henwood's belief that he was defending his friend and his friend's wife from von Phul and "Mrs. Springer's foolishness." He told the jury, "No one can have greater regret than this defendant at Mr. Copeland's death. Mr. Henwood is being tried for all intents and purposes for the killing of von Phul, and in order to convict him in the Copeland case you must believe beyond a reasonable doubt that he killed him intentionally." He asked for an acquittal. Henwood was moved to tears and dabbed at his eyes with a handkerchief.

Bottom's words had barely died away when Elliott tore into Henwood's defense. Speaking in a low voice, forcing the jury to listen closely, he said, "Frank Harold Henwood killed George E. Copeland and Tony von Phul. Why should one attempt to prove to this jury that black is white, just because white happens to be the side he is allied with? I, for one, shall not try it. It is an insult to the intelligence of this jury." There followed a brilliant summary of the evidence against Henwood—the bullet in von Phul's back; the fact that Springer never testified on Henwood's behalf; that Henwood himself said, "I shot Mr. von Phul. I intended to shoot Mr. von Phul. I knew what I was doing. I shot in self-defense"; and that Isabel Springer pleaded with him to withdraw. He scoffed at Henwood's contention that he acted only to save the Springers' marriage. "Mr. Chiles said, 'Henwood was taken into the bosom of the Springer family.' God! How literally true that statement was."

It was past 10 P.M. when Judge Whitford finally excused the exhausted jury, which had listened to testimony for twelve hours. He suggested that they get a good night's sleep before beginning their deliberations. By 9 A.M. the next day, the jury gathered in its second-floor room to begin deliberations. Rumors drifted to the crowds waiting outside that the jury already had decided that Henwood was guilty. The only question to be decided was to what degree. One observer claimed the vote almost immediately went to eight to four for first-degree murder. While they deliberated, bookmaker John Grim stood on the lawn between the courtroom and the jail, taking bets on the outcome. Most players were putting their money on first-degree murder. Others took a chance on second-degree murder. Few thought Henwood would be acquitted.

Meanwhile, Henwood waited in his cell. E.T.R., the warden's fox terrier, nestled in his arms. His friend Frank Loveland stopped by to offer support. The prisoner brushed dog hair off his blue serge suit as he talked with a small group of reporters. "He seems to know that there is something wrong," Henwood said of E.T.R. "He always comes to see me when I come back from the courtroom but this morning he is either trying to show me that he is glad I am staying in or that he feels I may take comfort in his presence."

Try as they might, the reporters could not get Henwood to talk specifically about the case, other than to say he was sure he would be acquitted and "that nothing was shown by the prosecution except what the spleen of a vindictive old woman [Cora Carpenter] against Mrs. Springer could inspire." He explained that because he still stood to be tried for killing von Phul, he couldn't talk about the case. His confidence that he would win acquittal was not wholehearted. "Naturally, I am as nervous as a bug on a stove. But out of this I have learned one thing—that is, who my friends are, the value of friendship." And still he waited.

When the jury returned from lunch at 2 P.M., all twelve men were in agreement. Informed that the jury, after only four hours of deliberation, had reached a decision, the bailiff called Judge Whitford and the attorneys to the courtroom. A few minutes before 3, everyone, including Henwood, had taken their places. Henwood, much of his bravura evaporated, looked around the room nervously and scanned the faces of the jurors, searching for a clue to his fate. Clerk William Rice asked jury foreman John Baxter, who amused other jurors during the trial with his habit of consuming three times a day a drink made of sugar, vinegar, and water, if they had reached a verdict. "We have."

The written verdict was handed to Judge Whitford, who took his glasses from his vest pocket, unsealed the envelope, read the note, and handed it to Rice. "Gentlemen," said Rice, "listen to the reading of your verdict." Henwood tensed, the color left his face. "We, the jury, find the defendant, Frank H. Henwood, guilty of murder in the second degree, as charged."

Henwood scarcely moved. He blinked rapidly and his lips quivered slightly, but he said nothing. Bottom was on his feet, demanding that members of the jury be polled individually. Each man was asked, "Was and is this your verdict?" Each said it was. Bottom made a brief attempt to have one of the jurors, Joseph Duval, disqualified because he once lived under a different name in Cripple Creek, but his protest was overruled. Thwarted, he told observers, "This case will be reversed. The verdict will not stand. We'll win yet."

❖

Crestfallen, Henwood was led back to his cell. On Banker's Row, where privileged prisoners were kept separated from the general prison population, in the west wing of the County Jail, he paced up and down the corridor all evening. At first he refused to talk about his trial, but then he shared with other prisoners his one opinion of what happened: "Whether she meant to or not, Mrs. Springer gave me the double cross. Her testimony, when she stated that I had 'butted in' on her affairs after she had told me not to, hurt me. It hurt me because it was with her consent that I tried to get those letters from von Phul."

Two days after the decision was announced, Isabel Springer's four-year marriage came to an end. Her aggrieved husband was granted a divorce, based on her disregard for their marital vows. The divorce settlement included her keeping her married name and her promise that she would leave Denver and never return. Before she left town, however, she fired both Carpenter and Lepper for their testimony that reflected on her character, leaving her brother, Arthur Patterson, in charge of the Cross Country Ranch.

She saved her harshest criticism for her maid, Irma Braasch, who supplied to Springer and his divorce attorneys much of the information on Isabel's nights with Henwood at the ranch and about her letters to von Phul. "Irma Braasch is a snake in the grass," she told *The Post*. "I hope no one will ever be so deceived in a maid as I was in her. I had her in my employment for over a year before I discovered what a viper she was and the poisonous effect of her sting. I consider Irma one of the immediate causes for my present unhappy condition."

Bottom launched a series of appeals based upon, among other things, the judge's denial of a continuance when the case began, Judge Whitford's claim that there was no manslaughter verdict possible, and various prejudicial remarks made by the judge in the presence of the jury. Henwood was due to be tried for the murder of von Phul, but Bottom claimed "former jeopardy," arguing that the two men's deaths were one incident. On July 26, only two days before Judge Whitford was to sentence Henwood for Copeland's death, Bottom appeared in court and recited ninety-one errors, reasons Henwood should be granted a new trial. He read through the long list and said he would produce a witness who would tell how he overheard a barroom conversation in which Judge Whitford referred to one of those who witnessed the shooting as "our star witness."

"I want to know, Mr. Bottom, on what information you as a lawyer base this charge?" Whitford interrupted.

"When I put it in there I believed it, your honor. If you and the district attorney will say that it is not true I will admit that it is not."

"I do not say it is not true. I am not called upon to say so. You have charged everyone connected with this trial, except for yourself and the defendant, with misconduct. As a man claiming to be a reputable lawyer, it is scandalous and unpro-fessional. I want to know who told you."

"I was told by someone."

"I ask you to tell me where you got your information."

"I will sometime later."

"You will tell the court now. I am talking to you as a lawyer claiming to be a reputable lawyer. You are standing there charging this court with misconduct."

"If your honor will allow me to consult with my client."

"You don't have to consult with your client."

"I don't think I can inform the court unless I consult with my client."

"Then you refuse to tell the court now. Mr. Bailiff, bring in the stenographer. It's a shame that any lawyer at this bar will stand before this court and read to him such charges and not have the courage to tell the court who told him. I want to know the source of your information, Mr. Bottom, but we will pass over the matter for the present and you may proceed with your reading."

"Yes, your honor. I should like to be heard later on that."

"You will not be heard later. The court will take up the matter, but the hearing is ended."

It was a veiled threat—a not very subtle one—that Judge Whitford would remember the conversation when the time came to decide Henwood's sentence.

For his part, Henwood continued to wear a public face of confidence. "We are going on a fishing trip when this is over, Mr. Bottom and I. I am not afraid to go up for my sentence, and I never have been."

He appeared before Judge Whitford for sentencing on July 28. Bottom asked for a delay until his appeal could be heard by the state Supreme Court but was turned down.

Facing Henwood, Judge Whitford said, "Have you anything to say why the court should not pronounce sentence on the verdict of the jury?"

"I have." Slowly, he walked to a water pitcher on the attorneys' table and poured himself a glass. He drank it slowly, then approached the railing in front of the prisoner's pen, his left hand resting lightly on the rail. His voice taut, he launched a vitriolic and angry diatribe at the judge. Despite the fact that his fate hung in the balance—Judge Whitford could give him a sentence that ranged from ten years to life—Henwood, who sat through ten days of a trial he thought unfair, went on for thirty minutes. Glancing from time to time at a small notebook, he said, in part,

Judge Whitford, I am not surprised that I am up here for sentence before you after the attitude you have taken toward me since this trial started. I have been over in this jail for perhaps two months. I have seen criminals, innocent men and others, afraid to come to trial before you because you hold the reputation of being a prejudiced judge, a biased judge—a man with a mind for just one thing, and that is conviction. A man is guilty before he enters this courtroom, in your estimation.

My idea of a judge is that he is fair and just to both sides. I never have had that justice from you; I never expected it after I heard you overrule my attorney one day—a good honest man who has had practically no money from me, who has put his hand in his own pocket to help me, who knows that thing against my honor is a lie and that the district attorney must know, in his own heart, although he is a prosecutor, that it is a lie.

When Mrs. Springer was on the stand she was not permitted to testify fully, but her testimony was held back, and you know it. The woman was put under morphine before she was put on the stand—and you know it and everybody knows it. The woman came on the stand here with a divorce hearing hanging over her head—a woman that had been shamed; her name had been in the papers, dragged through the dirt, and everything else.

I don't think it would make any difference how young my life was, if I were up here for sentence before you—it would make no difference. This is my personal opinion of you, Judge Whitford. From my observation, it does not make a bit of difference how young a life is or how old, whether man or woman, your one thought is, and always has been, conviction. You have been a prosecutor all your life and you know nothing else; it is like kleptomania with you, you have a desire to convict.

I have sat here to see my lawyer abused by you— I cannot call it anything else but abuse—you have allowed the district attorney to walk around and swagger through the courtroom and laugh out loud and criticize everybody, while my lawyer has been a gentleman since this trial started.

This is the first chance I have had to speak as a man would speak. I have noticed since I have been here that practically every day—almost every evening— you and the district attorney and his assistants go home in the same automobile together—go outside here and have some mutual understanding. I don't think that is right; I don't think it is right to the people of the state of Colorado. I know that you are going to pass sentence on me, which is the happiest part of this trial for you. I have not only been prosecuted, I have been persecuted.

I was not tried on the von Phul murder; I was not tried for shooting von Phul; I never murdered him. I shot him in self-defense, and everybody knows I did, and you never could have brought in a verdict of any-thing else but "not guilty" if you had tried me for the murder of von Phul. There is one thing that, as long as I live, I will spend everything I have got to wipe this thing off the slate—and you will help do it—call me the wrecker of the Springer home! Because, by God, I can't sleep at night. I can't do anything with that on my shoulders.

Judge Whitford, I cannot call you anything but a prosecuting judge. You should be called a prosecuting judge, you have been prosecutor on this bench; you have prosecuted me more so than the district attorney.

I stand ready for your unjust sentence.

No one spoke until Judge Whitford pointed out, in measured tones, that Henwood was surrounded in jail by men he had convicted. He explained how evidence convinced the jury that Henwood was guilty.

Henwood cut in. "May I interrupt?"

"No."

"In talking, I forgot something. You will ruin my case. I would like to . . ."

"Very well. I thought you were through. Say anything further that you want."

Henwood took up where he left off:

I believe it has been stated that I shot von Phul in the back. You have never shown that I shot von Phul in the back, and the evidence goes to show that the first shot might have struck him in the wrist. I am just as sure in my heart that the man was facing me as that I am facing you now, and that his first movement was to reach for his gun. The doctors brought by the state could not tell which direction the bullet went in his shoulder.

Now, there is not an American citizen who can satisfy himself in his own mind that after a man has struck a man and knocked him on the floor that [he] will immediately turn his back completely around. I have always claimed that the man was looking at me. I have always claimed that he put his hand on his hip pocket.

I think Mr. Chiles and Mr. Elliott will see the day when they are big enough to take me by the hand and say, when all of these things come out, that I have been wronged. All the truth is going to come out.

When Henwood stopped talking, Judge Whitford resumed, explaining that both attorneys believed Henwood was either guilty of murder or should be acquitted—"one extreme or the other"—and there was no in-between. The judge agreed with the attorneys. "The jury returned a verdict of second degree in the face of that testimony," he said. Then came the decisive moment. Judge Whitford looked down at the defiant Henwood and said,

I believe from what you have said that you shot purposely and with the intention of killing von Phul. I believe that you did it out of jealousy and revenge, excited by the passion that you entertained for the Springer woman, and that you shot to put von Phul out of the way; that you got your gun for that purpose. That being the case, the court being so advised, it would seem a case where the court, in the performance of its duty, ought to impose the maximum penalty under the law.

In this case, the judgment of the court is that you be confined in the penitentiary at Cañon City for and during your natural life.

Chapter Seven
ISABEL SPRINGER: "THE BUTTERFLY"

ONE BY THE ONE the petals fell from the blooms of the prim-rose path, to bring her at last into the tangle of thorns which snarled themselves at the end, which enmeshed her, tore at her with their poison-tipped lances, which dragged her downward, downward to the mire."

Courtney Ryley Cooper's flowery obituary on page one of *The Denver Post* on April 20, 1917, wrote an unglamorous finish to a decidedly glamorous woman. When she died in a New York City hospital charity ward, Isabel Patterson Springer was alone except for an actress friend.

In her lifetime, she rose to the top of Denver society, blessed with not one but three homes and showered with adulation. As the bride of John W. Springer, one of the city's most respected businessmen, she lived among the luxuries of the Brown Palace Hotel and the city's attractions, particularly the theater, which she attended frequently. She and her wealthy husband traveled widely, wintering in Pasadena, California, and visiting New York City often.

Isabel was a woman of charm and exceptional beauty, with large dark eyes and a soft, almost cherubic, countenance. She had a bountiful bosom and narrow waist of the type popular with turn-of-the-century women and their admirers. She preferred to wear her ample brown hair in the swept-up Gibson Girl style. Her dark eyebrows emphasized her piercing brown eyes. Her nose was more prominent than she might

Isabel Springer.
(Courtesy of the
Library of
Congress, LC-
USZ62-125674)

have liked, but it gave her face strength. She was born in 1880 to James and Amelia Evarts Patterson, either in Arkansas or in Michigan, both of which she claimed, at various times. As a child, she moved to St. Louis with her family and grew up in comfortable surroundings. Her family was among the city's social set.

In 1900, when she was only twenty years old, she married John E. Folck, a traveling shoe salesman. The couple moved to Memphis, Tennessee, but the marriage was unhappy almost from the beginning. Folck drank heavily and frequently pummeled her with abusive language and his fists. She was young, vibrant, and accustomed to the gay party life she had led in St. Louis. Her husband was frequently away from home, peddling footwear on the road in Missouri, Arkansas, and the Indian Territory. By June 1906, the two were separated.

Isabel moved back to St. Louis and took up residence in the Jefferson Hotel, center of the city's social scene. She was much in evidence among the gay set, earning the sobriquet

"The Butterfly" because of her fondness for attention and diversion. She and the wife of a wealthy St. Louisan were often observed cruising the city in the friend's eighty-horsepower touring car, "perhaps the finest then in St. Louis."

She was perceived to be the typical American girl, "chic, haughty, graceful and above all else, shatteringly pretty." Like other fashionable women, she wore her hair swept up, topped by outsized hats, blouses with huge sleeves, and long dresses with just the tiniest bit of ankle exposed. It was a style Isabel took to with flair.

When the twentieth century opened, many states forbade women the vote, the right to own property, or the right to claim their own earnings. In 1893, Colorado became the second state, after Wyoming, to grant women suffrage. By 1910, the suffrage movement was gaining power, although women wouldn't get the universal vote until the Nineteenth Amendment was ratified in 1920. But women already were beginning to move outside the home, driving automobiles, working in offices, and even smoking cigarettes. It was a time of great upheaval in American society. As Henry Allen noted in *What It Felt Like*, a decade-by-decade look at the twentieth century, "Women ignore their mothers' lessons on how a lady appears in public. They slowly jettison corsets, shed chaperones and hike their hemlines over their ankles. They face the camera with an amused wise guy wariness. Sometimes, for mischief, they pose with cigarettes. The face of sublimity starts to become the face of sexuality."

Isabel was clever with the opposite sex, like many of her peers who were accomplished at "dazzling their menfolk with feminine wiles." Though she was carefree and unconventional in her personal life, she was far from emancipated. After she married John Springer, this wealthy man took care of her worldly needs. She lived amidst maids, housekeepers, and chauffeurs. As a woman of leisure, she enjoyed ample time to read "romantic fiction that created an ideal of the softly genteel but indomitable female, and magazines that gave practical how-to instructions for achieving the ideal. Articles preached decorum and cautioned against dangerous new ideas." They were warnings she chose to ignore.

It was at the Jefferson Hotel that she met Springer and began her rise to the upper reaches of society. He was on his way to Kentucky to buy trotting horses when the two met. They hit if off immediately, and before summer's end in 1906 she was visiting him in Denver and was seen frequently on the city's streets, riding beside Springer in one of his finest coaches.

By that December, Isabel was in divorce court in St. Louis, seeking to end her marriage to Folck. She described Folck's abusive behavior, although she was unable to supply dates and places. Nevertheless, the judge, noting that her husband did not contest the divorce, made it official on December 23, leaving her free to pursue life with Springer. The two were married at the Jefferson on April 27, 1907, and left immediately for their new home in Denver.

❖

Isabel Springer arrived in a city that was shedding frontier dust and hardships. In the first decade of the twentieth century, Denver boasted fourteen parks covering twelve-hundred acres. There were two hundred miles of street railways, sixty hotels, twelve theaters, and sixty-five grade schools with more than thirty thousand pupils, and a hundred trains a day passed through the massive Denver Union Depot. There was a newly built U.S. Mint and a beautiful new public library. The city's streets, some paved, were swarming with an estimated two thousand of the newest plaything of the rich, the automobile, a sure sign of sophistication and wealth. For these motorists, Mayor Robert W. Speer had begun constructing an elaborate system of parkways. It wasn't St. Louis, but it wasn't the wild frontier either.

No sooner did Isabel arrive in the Queen City than newspaper society chroniclers were gushing over her. "We always thought John W. was pretty fair looking, but his wife is a stunning beauty, and it is safe to prophesy that the Springer home is going to be a social center." *Denver Post* columnist Eselyn Brown reported,

> Yesterday's bright sunshine brought forth a fine parade of automobiles and harness vehicles. Who failed to see the grand and shiny dogcart which traveled up and down Sixteenth Street just when the crowd was thickest? It looked as good as candied cherries and the color tallied exactly, too. The man who handled the reins wore an air of "See the conquering hero comes," and the lady at his side was a sight to behold. Just as you are asking yourself, "Whence comes all this grandeur?" the handsome man in a perfect fashion-plate outfit of the new leather brown shade clothes, turns his radiant face toward you, and, behold, it is John W. Springer. So the stunning lady at his side is the new Mrs. Springer? Well, she certainly is as queenly and beautiful as a three-sheet poster of Lillian Russell.

Isabel's life in Denver was idyllic. In addition to overseeing her castle-like home on Springer's ranch, she was mistress of the couple's two-story mansion at 930 Washington Street. She fit smoothly into the city's party circuit. Her name didn't appear in the society columns for luncheons and bridge tournaments, however; most of the social functions that she and John attended, outside of theater parties, were connected with politics and politicians. She was part of the elevated level of Denver society. A year after her arrival in Denver, she was a guest at a reception for the wife of the governor of Wyoming. The guests also included the wives of Messrs.

Guggenheim, Sheedy, Keating, and Kistler, all noteworthy Denver society names. Her dinner parties at the couple's suite on the sixth floor of the Brown Palace were renowned, particularly for the vintage wines poured. But Isabel's lust for adventure already was tugging at her.

Isabel was featured in the report in the *Rocky Mountain News* on society's coming out for the opening night of the *Follies of 1910* at the Broadway Theater. "Mrs. John W. Springer was one of the most strikingly beautiful women in the house and with her was Miss Louise Cherry, tall, graceful and blonde. Mr. and Mrs. Springer had a box party. Beside Miss Cherry in their box were H. F. Henwood and Frank Loveland." The Springers and Henwood had become fast friends after Isabel met Henwood in her husband's downtown office in March 1911. Weeks later, Henwood and Isabel were visiting the Springer ranch regularly, sometimes without Mr. Springer.

Springer traveled frequently for his banking, cattle, and other business interests and sometimes took his young bride with him to New York. It looked like heaven to the lively and impetuous Isabel. In New York, she fell in with a group of bohemians and began living a life she dared not mention. She was drinking heavily, using drugs, and even was known to pose nude for the city's artists. Her behavior at home was equally liberated. She had left one ardent admirer, Tony von Phul, in St. Louis, and had taken up with another, Frank Henwood, in Denver. It was inevitable the two men would clash.

When Henwood gunned down von Phul in the barroom of the Brown Palace on May 24, 1911, Isabel's life began to unravel. Despite attempts to keep her name out of the shooting incident and out of the local press, less than a week passed before her connection popped up in print. Her husband, having seen passionate letters she penned to von Phul, began divorce proceedings. On June 5, Springer's attorney, Archie M. Stevenson, filed the divorce suit in district court. Already humiliated by having his name dragged through the public prints, Springer denied to the press that he had filed, or that he planned to. "Emphatically no," he told *The Denver Republican*. But it was true.

His complaint charged Isabel with "wholly disregarding her marital vows" and said she "has been guilty of extreme and repeated acts of cruelty toward the plaintiff." It went on to charge that "for many months prior to the 20th day of May 1911, the defendant was engaged in an unwifely and clandestine correspondence with one Sylvester Louis von Phul." The letters were specifically mentioned, "letters…of such a character as to render the continuance of the marriage relation…impossible and intolerable." He was embarrassed.

When the existence of her letters became public, Isabel fled to Chicago, in part because of fears that she would be called as a witness for Henwood in his trial, which was to begin on June 21. She returned to Denver on June 11, hoping for a reconciliation with her banker husband. What followed was little more than a settlement negotiated in the public prints. She took apartments on the fifth floor of the Savoy Hotel, the same place she had stayed when she visited Springer in the summer of 1906. One of her attorneys, George A. H. Fraser, proclaimed, "The sole object of her return was to effect a reconciliation with Mr. Springer and the first conferences along that line were held this morning." Springer was uninterested in a reconciliation. His attorneys warned that if Isabel contested the divorce she would be cut off without a financial settlement.

Isabel and John never again met face-to-face, then or ever. He pointedly remained out of town or at his ranch and ignored her lawyers' letters sent to his offices. The couple's lawyers, however, negotiated for several weeks. In what was merely a legal shadow dance, Springer was granted a divorce on July 1, a Saturday morning, in the chambers of District Court Judge George W. Allen. The hearing lasted barely fifteen minutes. The settlement had been reached the previous evening, and it only remained for Springer to take the stand in front of his attorney Stevenson, Isabel's attorneys John T. Barnett and Daniel B. Ellis, Deputy District Attorney Dewey C. Bailey Jr., and Springer's friend, Dr. Charles Heberton, and recite his grievances. Both sides agreed to withhold the letters and other damaging (to Springer's standing in the community) evidence. A substitute decree, listing only the charges, was filed.

Isabel's problems were piling up. While divorce negotiations were going on, Sheriff William Arnett served her with a subpoena on June 14 to appear in court on behalf of the defense in Henwood's first trial. Arnett described her as "greatly overwrought" and "decidedly hysterical" when she was served. "She was very hysterical and cried nearly all the time, but promised to appear in court to testify when the time comes." She did appear, testifying on June 23 and June 26 for Henwood, but doing his case little good with disjointed and rambling testimony that emphasized her attempts to get him to withdraw from her affairs.

After the divorce was settled, the *Rocky Mountain News* reported what Mrs. Springer asked for and what she received in the settlement. She sought, according to the News, twenty-five thousand dollars in cash; her favorite automobile, a five-thousand-dollar Victoria; her diamonds and other jewelry; and the right to remain Mrs. John W. Springer. She received something less: only five thousand dollars in cash, the car (which she sold back to Springer for twenty-seven hundred dollars the following October), her jewels, her personal property, and his name. And she was to leave Denver immediately and never return.

She wasted no time leaving. Five hours after the court settlement, Isabel departed her hotel and took a taxi to the Union Depot, where she boarded the Burlington's luxury Chicago Limited. Her outfit would have looked familiar to anyone who had seen her on the witness stand at Henwood's first trial. She was wearing the same blue serge suit with a white lace collar, a veil covering her face, and she carried a black velvet bag.

Arthur Patterson, her brother, and Elizabeth Speers, her nurse, followed her to the depot in a separate cab and helped her board her stateroom in the Pullman car Pantheon. The shades were pulled to prevent the public and, more pointedly, reporters from looking in on her. Patterson stayed with his sister in her room until the train got under way at 3:45 P.M. As it slowly passed Nineteenth Street, he jumped off. Isabel was gone.

❖

As a young woman, Isabel Springer possessed beauty and wealth. But she had one flaw on a grand scale—she had terrible taste in men. Her first husband was a drinker and abusive. Her second husband, Springer, was an egocentric horseman and entrepreneur who fancied himself a politician. Her relationship with von Phul was marked by physical abuse and, ultimately, his threat to expose their relationship to her husband. Henwood was a charming ne'er-do-well who immediately won her over with his familiarities and outgoing demeanor. Her passionate letters to von Phul reveal an insecure woman seeking constant reassurance. "Why don't you write to your little sweetheart?" she asked. "You can't imagine how I have longed for you." And, "You know I am expecting a letter." She was susceptible to flattery and frequently remarked to her friends how Mr. So-and-So found her attractive.

Following her divorce from Springer and the hasty departure from Denver, she spent two years in Chicago, where she took to wearing white hair to hide her identity—a ploy that didn't disguise her but made her look old. Isabel made her way back to New York City in 1913 and resumed her life of dissipation. But she was no longer a doe-eyed young beauty.

She looked much older than her thirty-three years. A tiredness surrounded her once-riveting eyes. She had fast-forwarded to middle age. Years of drinking and drug abuse had taken their toll, adding pounds to her figure and years to her once-classic face.

As she did wherever she went, Isabel quickly made friends in New York, among them Audrey Munson, the city's leading model, whose face and figure were the inspirations for more than thirty nude public sculptures, including those at the Hotel Astor, the Municipal Building, the Custom House, and the New York Public Library. Her likeness adorned the Mercury Head dime and the Walking Liberty half-dollar. Munson was a star; Isabel was never more than a bit player.

When Munson's career began to wane in 1921, she wrote "Queen of the Artists' Studios," a series of supposedly tell-all articles for the *New York American* newspaper. The tales, largely woven from whole cloth and self-serving to Munson, were distributed to newspapers nationwide, including *The Denver Post*, once Isabel's hometown paper.

Readers of the Sunday supplements devoured the accounts of Munson's artistic life in New York. In one installment, she claimed that the murders at the Brown Palace were over a nude painting of Mrs. Springer, executed during her lively times in New York. In Munson's version, someone (apparently von Phul) threatened to show the painting to Isabel's husband unless she paid him hush money. After Isabel died, Munson wrote, a small circle of Isabel's friends "went to [her] rooming house and watched while the painting was burned." No other evidence exists that points either to the painting or to its fiery demise as related in Munson's superheated stories.

Munson dispensed one piece of advice that the adventuresome Isabel would have done well to follow. "Girls who go to the studios to pose thinking it fun and a nice diversion will soon find their mistake. It is hard work and the girls who fail

Isabel Springer, her legendary beauty battered by drugs and alcohol, wore her hair white after leaving Denver for Chicago, circa 1915. (Courtesy of the Library of Congress, LC-USZ62-75444)

are generally those who are not sincere," she wrote. "How can a woman be a bacchante all night and become an angel at ten o'clock in the morning?" She summed up Isabel's desperate efforts to carve a career for herself: "She sought work in respectable studios as a model for the nude. Here and there an artist took pity upon the fallen woman and engaged her, but none found her satisfactory because the woman who uses opium cannot hold a pose with necessary firmness."

Isabel was far from alone in her addictions. "An entire industry supplied nerve tonics, blood builders, sedatives and bromides for women," H. Wayne Morgan noted in *Yesterday's Addicts,* his study of drug abuse. "The invalid was a kind of heroine. But 'the vapors' or 'la Nervose' which became a way of life for many matrons rested also on social pressures and inhibitions. Middle-class women had few accepted outlets for aggression, tension and frustration, which increased the temptation to use drugs or alcohol to relieve boredom and anxiety." It was estimated that there were three hundred thousand addicts in New York City in 1917. In Denver, estimates of those addicted to cocaine and morphine varied wildly, ranging up to five thousand. It was an environment where prescriptions for morphine were available for fifty cents before 6 P.M. and seventy-five cents before midnight.

Opium and morphine were the drugs of choice. They were used readily in a variety of cough syrups, tonics, elixirs, and cure-alls to promote a sense of well-being. Drugs even made their way into the upper reaches of society. In *Menace in the West*, his survey of drug use in Colorado, Henry O. Whiteside wrote, "Ambitious and hardworking men, including doctors, lawyers and even ministers, used drugs to overcome fatigue and then to bring sleep. But among 'opium eaters' or drinkers, women were believed to outnumber men by a margin of greater than ten to one." One reason advanced was that while women tended to remain homebound, men were able to frequent saloons and imbibe equally relaxing amounts of cheap whiskey and lager beer.

Her health declining rapidly, and left destitute by medical bills, Isabel was admitted to Metropolitan Hospital on Blackwell's Island in New York City on March 28, 1917. In a lonely bed in the charity ward, death came to her in the middle of the night on April 19. Her death certificate gives evidence that Isabel Springer was doing more with her body than posing unclothed for the "Titians of the attics." The official cause of death was ruled to be "cirrhosis of liver (hypertrophic)," an enlargement that indicated a longtime abuse of alcohol. A contributory cause was "alcoholic neuritis."

She almost certainly was also addicted to opium and/or morphine, the latter a habit she may have shared with Henwood. Only one friend, an actress with whom she had worked, was at her side when she died near midnight.

Perhaps it was Isabel herself who, in her dying days, gave the information found on her death certificate because both her parents' names (and her mother's maiden name) are listed. The death certificate listed her age as thirty-one and her status as married. She was neither.

Isabel, who long ago had spent her way through the divorce settlement she received in 1911 and had earned a bare living with bit parts in silent pictures and by posing for artists, was penniless. When she died, she was living in a rooming house at 343 St. Nicholas Avenue. According to Munson's memoir, "In her meager effects, strewn about in the sordid rooming house where she had found shelter, there was nothing that could be sold for enough to provide even a casket for the Potter's Field."

Her body went unclaimed, and she seemed destined to an anonymous burial. Telegrams to her brother, Arthur Patterson, and to her former husband, John Springer, went unanswered. A few of her New York friends, including theatrical producer William A. Brady, musical comedy star Kitty Gordon, and actress Eileen Fredericks, donated enough money for her to be buried on April 23, 1917, at Fair View Cemetery in Fairview, Bergen County, New Jersey. The high-spirited woman whose beauty was praised universally, who became the belle of Denver society, for whom an admirer killed two men, had no monument to mark her burial plot.

Her death attracted no notice in the New York newspapers, but famed evangelist Billy Sunday was moved enough by her demise to tell a crowd of twenty thousand during a series of revival meetings at his New York tabernacle, "Take warning from the fate of Mrs. John W. Springer. A few years ago she was a society woman, with all the jewels and trappings that go with society women. A day or two ago she died a pauper at Blackwell's Island. Sin did that. She used to be called one of the most beautiful women in the United States or Europe." And, he said, "I knew her when she was in Denver, and when she was the pet of international society. She had great wealth and a palatial home. But she yielded to sin, the sin of society; she drank at hotels and cafes."

Reporters descended on John Springer, still a well-known figure in Denver. He declined comment on the death of his former wife. "I have nothing at all to say," he told the *Rocky Mountain News.* "If you were to consult my wishes, you would say nothing at all about it."

When told in his prison cell at the state penitentiary in Cañon City about Isabel's death, Henwood showed little emotion. "I have not heard anything whatever of the whereabouts of Mrs. Springer or anything in connection with her or her movements since the unfortunate occurrence in the Brown Hotel in Denver. I am very sorry to hear of her death."

He could not, however, hide the bitterness of her betrayal at his trials. "The shooting at the hotel was due to my efforts to save Mrs. Springer from a man I considered thoroughly immoral, but evidently the lesson of that tragedy was not heeded. She went the way so many women do when once they start on the primrose path. I realize now that I should not have interfered in any way." Unforgiving, he concluded, "Death has sealed the lips and silenced the voice that might have done so much to help me get out of prison."

Isabel Springer was not entirely forgotten in Denver. In the wake of her passing, the *News* published a lengthy editorial, headlined "The Wages of Sin," without once mentioning her by name. It read, in part,

> Her fame had departed, her beauty was no more. She had wasted her natural endowments in riotous living. The story is as old as original sin. Nature had been prodigal to the woman. She was not only good to look upon, she had brains and knew how to use them. She was held to blame. Those who were without sin and those who had sinned cast the first and last stone at her;

she was a vampire, an outcast that could not from that time forward reach the fringes of "society." She was the haunted woman. The descent to Avernus is steep we are told and there is not room for a woman to turn back. Down, down it must be. The wages of sin is death.

Two women reporters, ones who had exclaimed over her beauty and grace when she reigned as John Springer's wife, expressed in print what many in society whispered into their teacups.

Alice Rohe of the *News* cited vamps throughout history, including the obscure Thaïs, to show her disapproval. "It is when woman begins to enthrall men without intellect, but through sheer physical lures and sex attractions that she descends from the class of great courtesans into the mire of unnameable creatures. And when women sin for the mere gratification of their desires, the somber saying that the wages of sin is death sound truer than ever."

Reporter Frances Wayne said of the beguiling Isabel,

Mrs. Springer was very pretty and oh! so feminine! She had charm. She was never heard to say disagreeable things about anybody; she had the smartest turnouts in town; she wore the most stunning frocks; her hats were miracles, and her dinners—her dinners provided the finest wine the palate could desire. Mrs. Springer was tender, and gentle and very, very sympathetic. Her tips to servants were the talk of the hotel. Sometimes Mrs. Springer stormed and raved—but then a lady must occasionally prove her temperament is not dulled—even by marriage.

She was thirty-seven years old when she died.

Chapter Eight
THE REASON: "FOOLISH LITTLE LETTERS"

WHEN FRANK HENWOOD'S blazing pistol sprayed death in the barroom of the Brown Palace, the real smoking gun lay in the pocket and rooms of Tony von Phul. It consisted of a series of letters, some of them quite passionate, that Isabel Patterson Springer wrote to von Phul during the first five months of 1911. The letters became the focal point of the dispute between von Phul and Henwood. Von Phul, Isabel told Henwood, threatened to show the letters to her husband, and she asked Henwood to get them back, a request she later claimed in court that she asked him to ignore.

They were of such an intimate nature that her husband filed for divorce in Denver District Court four days after he read the letters and his wife's involvement in the dispute became public.

Members of the city's high society were stunned by the revelations that slowly came to light. Particularly disturbing was "the utter disregard of conventions showed by Mrs. Springer in her affairs," huffed *Rocky Mountain News* columnist Alice Rohe. "A woman who tossed the real things of life like a house of cards, who wrought her own downfall—the presence of Mrs. Springer in the Henwood case would bring an element of moral teaching which is the repetition of such affairs since man and woman became mad with the folly of irregular liaisons."

The Denver Post's Frances Wayne painted Isabel as a "man eater," a seducer, not unlike many young women who manipulate men. "The easiest way they have found is to assume the 'eternal feminine' pose. The voice is turned into a soft coo, the eyes lift slowly, their animation is that of the perfume rising from a flower, rather than flame from fire. There is nothing obviously exhausting about these women."

Of the many aspects of the legal proceedings, none attracted more attention than did the letters and telegrams sent by Isabel Springer to Tony von Phul. Found by authorities after von Phul's death, they were written between January 31 and May 20 of 1911. They showed, said *The Post* on June 16, 1913, during Henwood's second trial, "that Mrs. Springer enjoyed the most friendly relations with Von Phul." The next day, the paper, practically blushing, printed portions of some of the letters, noting, "Incidents in which Von Phul and Mrs. Springer figured are referred to constantly in them, meetings in St. Louis and Hot Springs [Arkansas], and the language—well, it's hardly printable."

After their discovery in von Phul's effects, the letters became well traveled. Found by police, they were turned over to the coroner and then to the district attorney's office. Copies were made, and they began turning up in the hands of various lawyers, including Henwood's, Springer's, and the prosecutors. How some of the letters, and portions of others, made it into the news columns, where they were read eagerly by an enthralled public, is uncertain. Springer read the letters a week after the shooting because he was close friends with then-District Attorney Willis V. Elliott, who prosecuted the 1911 case against Henwood. Elliott and Springer agreed that the letters should not be made public because of the damage they would wreak on the wealthy Springer's stature in the community. They were locked up in the district attorney's office.

Elliott left office in the fall of 1912, then died unexpectedly in Wiggins, Colorado, while on a business trip in May 1913. He was succeeded as district attorney by John A. Rush, who inherited the job and the letters. When they reached print, mainly in *The Denver Republican* in 1913, Springer told the paper, "So far as I can learn positively, there are no known copies of the letters extant." He did not sound totally convinced because he also said, "It is presumed that some person had managed to get hold of some of the letters long enough to make three or four copies of each before he was detected." He implied that attorney Rush had broken a trust by revealing the letters' contents to enhance his case, proving Isabel to be an unfaithful wife. Rush, also a friend of Springer's, was offended. "One thing is absolutely certain, and that is that no human eye has seen either the originals or any copy of any of the letters turned over to me. They have been locked up where no one has seen them, and Mr. Springer could have ascertained that fact with the slight trouble of asking me."

His friendship with Springer did not prevent Rush from using the threat of reading the letters into the court record during Henwood's second trial to keep Isabel from testifying on Henwood's behalf. "I shall be compelled to produce the letters in open court. I respect friendships and have done nothing to violate this one, yet I shall not allow that fact to deter me from doing my full duty in bringing justice to a man like Henwood."

There seemed to be a good many letters from Isabel to von Phul floating around. After his death, von Phul's sister in St. Louis, Mrs. Marie Kimbrough, talked about an altogether different set of letters:

> Members of our family in St. Louis upbraided Tony for his association with Mrs. Springer, but for a time he was infatuated with her. He learned his mistake and then she began writing him those letters which we have in our possession. She pleaded with him until he resumed his relations with her. In St. Louis she quarreled with him and after she became acquainted with Henwood she wrote Tony, asking

him to send back her letters. He did not take the matter seriously and did not take the trouble to get the letters together. Mrs. Springer then wrote Tony, asking him to go to Denver. We believe that at the same time Henwood understood that he could do Mrs. Springer a great service by recovering the letters.

Detectives who searched von Phul's pockets also found a small black leather notebook which contained addresses of women—many of them actresses and many of them with the prefix "Mrs."—with whom he had been intimate. Among the names in his book was Mrs. Isabel Patterson Springer, followed by the inscription, "Florence E. Welch, 619 East Sixth Avenue, Denver. Mark X on back." Welch was Isabel's manicurist, confidante, and the intermediary for von Phul's letters. The X was a code that identified letters he sent to Welch that were intended for Mrs. Springer.

The bulk of the letters and telegrams exchanged were never made public. The city's four daily newspapers, perhaps reluctant to offend their readers' sensibilities, printed portions of some letters and only salutations and dates of others. The letters have not surfaced since they were locked away in 1913.

❖

The following letters and excerpts of letters from Isabel to von Phul were gleaned from newspapers of the day. They served their purpose for the prosecution—Isabel Patterson Springer, who left Denver in 1911 for the East, did not return.

January 31, 1911 (partial letter)
Dearest Love—
    I can hardly bear to be away from you I miss you so much. You are the only one I love in the world.
    Isabel

A few days later, unable to persuade von Phul to come to Denver, Isabel told him that she would visit him in Kansas City, where he was on business with his wine company. She expressed her concern about his career as a balloonist, urging him to follow her advice "and stay on the ground." She was so taken with von Phul that she risked writing to him while her husband was waiting in the next room at their Brown Palace suite to take her to dinner.

[Date unknown]
Sweetheart,

Why don't you write to your little sweetheart? It has been three days since I had a line from you, and I am nearly crazy. I have been worrying myself to death for fear something has happened to you. If I don't get a letter or some word from you within the next twenty-four hours I will take the first train to Kansas City, so my little sweetheart can hold me in his arms.

Did you make the balloon trip? Or did you take my advice and stay on the ground? I am always worried when you are in the sky, for fear something will happen.

John is in the next room waiting for me to finish this letter, so we can go to dinner. He thinks I am writing to mother.

I feel pretty good again, but yesterday I was sick. You know what the trouble is this time, don't you, dear?

I must go to dinner with John, so will close, hoping to hear from you in the morning. With lots of love and kisses,

Yours till the end,
Isabel

The following day, she telegraphed von Phul and repeated her warning:

[Date unknown]

No letter came this morning when Florence [Welch] come to the hotel. If I don't hear from you at once I will leave for Kansas City.

Lots of love,
Isabel

Her next letter, written on Mercy Hospital stationery on February 6, began, "My Own Precious" and told of her impending surgery.

Between February and April, she suffered a series of medical problems, which she didn't hesitate to relate with some drama. This trip to the hospital would be followed by another, and she described various ailments she had been troubled with. A note written a few days later from Mercy Hospital just before her surgery reflected her concern and seriousness of the operation, the nature of which was never explained. In the beginning of the letter, she joked about taking "an automobile ride," but as she wound up the note, she turned serious, asking von Phul to "remember that you are the only one I ever loved." Her mention to von Phul that "you know what the trouble is" and her sudden surgery only days later hints at something other than appendicitis.

February 12
My Darling—

They are waiting in the hall with that funny little cart on which I am going to take an automobile ride, to take me to the operating room. John, brother [Arthur Patterson] and the rest of them are sitting in another room worrying themselves to death about my condition, but, dear, you are the only one I am interested in, and if they only knew.

I must cut this short, for the men are waiting in the hall and the nurse is standing in the room, waiting for me to finish this letter to take me to the operating room.

Well, dear, if I don't come out of this and if I never see you again, just remember that you are the only one I ever loved.

Isabel

Letters followed every few days and by March 27 she was writing from Hot Springs, Arkansas. A second surgery, reported by one paper to be an appendectomy, followed when she returned to Denver in mid-April.

February 13

My Sweetheart—

No letter came today and I was so disappointed the nurses became alarmed. Florence came to see me, but I felt so disappointed that she did not stay but a few minutes.

Isabel

Only the salutations of a series of letters written between February 15 and April 13 were reprinted by the newspapers. Most began "Dearest" and were signed "Isabel."

April 1911

My Darling—

Just a little note tonight to let you know your little sweetheart is thinking of you. John is in the next room and likely to come in at any minute, so you know I must hurry.

Oh, how I wish you were here tonight to tuck me in my little bed and kiss me goodnight. I have been sick ever since I left St. Louis and you can't imagine how I have longed for you, sweetheart. It seems that something is always the matter with me. First I was in Mercy Hospital for that old operation, then I was laid up with the grippe, and now . . .

It is just one thing after another and if I continue to be ill I shall try and persuade John to let me go to Hot Springs. Then I can see you and be with you, sweetheart. When do you expect to come to Denver? Some time soon, I hope. Unless you make arrangements to come here I shall leave for St. Louis within the next four weeks.

Must close now as I hear John moving about in the next room. Florence is coming tomorrow and you know I am expecting a letter. If I fail to get one, you know I shall be disappointed.

Hurriedly,

Isabel

April 1911

Sweetheart—

The operation is over and it was successful. I am beginning to feel like myself again. Yesterday the doctor took out the stitches, and, oh, sweetheart, how it did hurt. I didn't cry because I knew you would call me a baby.

I am sending you a piece of one of the stitches which the doctor took out today. This is the longest one I could find and I told the nurse to be sure and save it for me because I wanted to send it away. She laughed at me, but I knew you would like to have it.

I will soon be out of the hospital and then I will tell John that a trip will be a good thing for me. I am sure he will let me go to the Hot Springs and then you can hold me in your arms once more and make me the happiest woman in the world.

With all the love in the world, and hoping to be with you soon, I am, yours forever,

Isabel

A few days later, she wrote again,

[Date unknown]

Sweetheart—

Just a few lines to let you know I am back to my hotel and I am more than glad to get away from that old hospital. I am beginning to feel fine again and to long for the time, dearie, when you can be with me.

How I wish you were here tonight to tuck me in my little bed and say nice things to me—things that no on else in the whole world could say and make me happy. How I am longing for the time to come when you can hold me in your arms again and pat me on the head and whisper tender things to me.

John don't think I am as well as I am, and I will keep him thinking that way. Then when I tell him I need a trip he will let me go back to Hot Springs so I can be near you.

Florence came to the hotel today, but no letter. You can't imagine how disappointed I was when she told me. But I suppose you have been busy, but you must remember that you must not forget your little sweetheart out here in Denver, who is pining and longing to be with you.

Just as soon as I can arrange it with John, I will go to Hot Springs. I will wire you when I leave Denver, so you can meet me there.

Must close now, as I expect John home any minute and I want to have this letter out of the way before he comes.

With all the love a woman is able to give, I am sending to you, the only man I have ever really loved.

Isabel

[Date unknown]

I have been looking at the incision today and I am very glad to find that it is not nearly as bad as I thought it was.

I was so afraid it would be bad and that it would leave an ugly scar and that you would not like it. But I believe everything is going to be all right and that I am not going to be ugly. But you will not mind the scar, will you?

You know, dear, that you promised to love me and to love the scar, and you must keep your promise.

Isabel

Part of a telegram sent to von Phul while she was in Hot Springs:

[Date unknown]

I was very disappointed when I went to bed last night, because I did not hear from you. I waited up until very late expecting a telephone [call] from you. …Be sure and phone me today.

With lots of love and kisses.

Isabel

The correspondence was ardent and frequent.

[Date unknown, probably mid-May]
Dear Tony Boy,

I did not get your message until yesterday. I had a frightful headache last night and could not answer you until today.

I am very sorry you feel the way you do, and Dear Boy, I must assure you you are wrong—wrong—wrong.

I want you to give up that trip and come here directly. I shall expect you here in a week and no later. I want you here and you must come. If you do I will tell you what you will be glad to hear, something I cannot put down here. There are reasons why you should at least postpone your trip and you will be glad you came.

Frank is still here, and is, of course, still acting naughty.

I have quite a surprise in store for you—something that will please you I am sure, and the other will be all adjusted as soon as you arrive and you will be yourself again.

I heard from A. last week. He told me what you had said and I am glad you told me first. A. is all right, but—well, you understand. We were out of town day before yesterday and you were spoke of frequently.

You must come directly here as soon as you arrive and I will share your surprise with you. Cora was in town Saturday and Mrs. C and I were with her and F. all afternoon. She should be here [there?] by this time—perhaps you have seen her. She will be in Denver again next week. You will find us quite merry and there will not be the same affair as that of a month ago. I still watch out for that and you shall help me. V. is still here and asks for you often.

I shall expect you, Tony, next week. Wire me if you cannot come, and wire me when you start. The other matter will be satisfactorily arranged you may be sure. So, until I get your wire, as always,

Belle

Why Isabel would mention Frank Henwood's attentions to her in this letter remains a mystery, although she liked to point out that men found her attractive.

❖

Only one of von Phul's letters to Isabel was published. It was written shortly before he left Kansas City for Denver and was sent, as usual, via Florence Welch, who passed it on to Isabel, who sent it via her maid to Henwood without opening it because Henwood had told her a few days earlier that she must no longer communicate with von Phul. Isabel was nothing if not accommodating. The date it was written is unknown. Henwood's defense attorneys point to the line "just show him where he gets off or I will" as proof that von Phul had murderous intentions toward Henwood when he came to town. The signature, "M," was von Phul's code name. He also signed his letters "Mabel."

[Date unknown]
    If you are too busy to write me a letter, just say so and I won't expect them. I have not heard from you for three days. I leave here about the 23rd for Denver, if [my] father does not die, but I am afraid the old man is in pretty bad condition and am holding myself in readiness for a quick trip home. The least I expect from you is for you to behave yourself while I am under this terrific strain, and have nothing to do with that double crosser. No, you don't have to take him out to the ranch or have anything to do with him— just show him where he gets off or I will.
    M

Isabel sent frequent telegrams to von Phul, all of which expressed her love for him. "I love you better than anyone else. I belong all to you, as you already know," read one.

Even more desperate was one she sent on May 20, only three days before he arrived in Denver for the final countdown to his death. "For God's sake, wire me. I can't stand your silence any longer. I am crazy to see and be with you. You know what my answer will be when you come. Isabel."

What Tony's question was cannot be known for sure, but her promises helped compel the St. Louis aeronaut to ignore his father's ill health and rush to Denver.

It is unclear why von Phul warned Isabel—according to what she told Henwood—that he would show the letters to her husband unless she resumed their St. Louis romance. Von Phul certainly wasn't happy with the appearance of Henwood in Isabel's life. There were various rumors and theories. In the days following the shooting, friends of von Phul claimed that Henwood conspired with "a Denver society woman" to plot von Phul's murder. "Mr. von Phul was not a barroom fighter or a drunkard." Both Springer and von Phul pursued Isabel while she was living at the Jefferson Hotel in St. Louis following her separation from her first husband, and von Phul may have been angry that she chose to marry the millionaire businessman instead of a balloon-riding adventurer. A conspiracy theorist could hypothesize that Isabel, experienced in the ways of men, plotted to prod Henwood into killing von Phul, thus freeing her of both suitors.

Certainly, von Phul could not have been threatening her with exposure because she was breaking off their relationship. She wasn't. Beginning in January, she repeatedly pleaded with him to visit her in Denver, reminding him that "your little sweetheart is thinking of you." In mid-May, she wrote, "I want you here and you must come. If you do I will tell you what you will be glad to hear...." And just days before he arrived at the Brown Palace, she telegraphed, "I love you better than anyone else." Not the words of a woman who wanted to end an affair.

Most likely is that von Phul resented the sudden appearance in Isabel's life of the wandering gas salesman, Henwood. His visits to the Springer ranch, the trips to the theater, and the elaborate parties at the Springer hotel suite, at which he was a guest, must have infuriated von Phul, who was hearing love from Isabel but seeing evidence that he was not the only love in her life. He had her "foolish little letters" and, having already proved himself a bully, would not have hesitated to use them to bring her back into line. His jealousy proved to be his undoing.

Chapter Nine
A Second Chance: "I've Got a New Trial"

Frank Henwood could not have picked a worse time or place to commit mayhem.

Denver, barely a half-century old, survived a shaky frontier beginning, droughts, fires, floods, arsonists, gunslingers, crooked politicians, swindlers, and murderers. The economic collapse of 1893 was a distant memory. By the second decade of the new century, a sense of reform gripped the Queen City of the Plains. Murders and high-society peccadilloes did not fit in with the vision of its forward-looking and civic-minded citizens. Two particularly sensational murder cases within six months raised their ire. The shooting at the Brown Palace in May 1911 followed an equally sensational case in which a young housewife, Gertrude Gibson Patterson, shot her abusive husband in the back in late 1910, then claimed he committed suicide. A last-minute, mystery witness testified that he had seen the shooting, which occurred after Mrs. Patterson's husband struck her several times. She was acquitted.

The Reverend H. Martyn Hart, dean of the Cathedral of St. John in the Wilderness, spoke for many in July 1911 when he denounced in a sermon men and women taking the law into their own hands. "America generally is rotten with this sort of crime, and it is high time that something was done to arrest it before it becomes too late. When will Denver be freed from the blot which now rests upon its name? Unavenged, the blood of more than a score of unfortunate men—murdered within this city—is calling for retribution."

The Post, which thrived on vivid accounts of crimes with equally vivid headlines, thundered in a page-one editorial two days after the Brown Palace incident, "This gun-toting habit is getting to be such a fierce and uncontrollable proposition that the police do not seem able to cope with it. [If] this indiscriminate mowing down of human beings continues... something may happen that Denver will regret far more than an ordinary murder or two. It must be taken for granted that a man who carries a revolver means to use it."

Author Upton Sinclair, muckraker and Socialist, had little patience with the upper classes or with the newspapers that reported on their daily lives and transgressions.

It goes on, and everybody in the hotels knows that it is going on, including the management of the hotels; but do you read anything about it in the newspapers? Only when it gets into the law courts; and then you get only the personal details—never the philosophy of it. Never are such facts used to prove that the capitalist system is a source of debauchery, prostitution, drunkenness and disease; that it breaks up the home, and makes true religion and virtue impossible!

For the most part what you read about these leisure-class hotels in the newspapers is elaborate advertisement of the hotels and their attractions, together with fatuous and servile accounts of the social doings of the guests: columns and columns of stuff about them, what they eat and what they drink and what they wear, what games they play and what trophies they win, how much money they have, and what important positions they fill in the world, and their opinions on every subject from politics to ping-pong. They are "society."

The city's growing population yearned for respectability. They were an enthusiastic part of a nationwide campaign known as the moral uplift movement. A new breed of politicians and a stringent rewriting of ordinances would shut down Denver's thriving red-light district and curtail licenses and locations for saloons. Under Mayor Robert W. Speer, huge civic improvements would be made, including the building of Civic Center and the creation of parks and the planting of thousands of trees.

So fervent was the rush to morality that a visiting federal judge was moved to plead against using the courts to enforce morality instead of laws. Three weeks before the shootings at the Brown Palace, Judge Robert E. Lewis warned, "The moral uplift movements of the present day prompt men to accuse other men of crimes on the slightest pretext. The courts of the land have nothing to do with regulating the morals of the people."

❖

When Henwood blew into Denver late in 1910, he immediately became part of Denver society, partly because he had grown up in well-to-do circumstances and enjoyed the high life and partly because he was desperate to forge a new career for himself and needed monied contacts to finance his new enterprise as a promoter for the gas company. It was his friend and business partner, Frank Loveland, who helped him. Loveland made sure Henwood met the right people. "Ever since Henwood first came to Denver I have known him about as well as anyone ever did," Loveland liked to brag. "I have introduced him to a number of people. Mr. Springer liked him very much and as Mrs. Springer does a great deal of entertaining and whatever entertaining is done in the family is done by her, Henwood was often seen with her. Never, however, without Mr. Springer."

Widely traveled, Henwood fit in easily into his new environment. One observer noted,

> That he comes of people of breeding and culture is manifest even upon short acquaintance. He has all the earmarks that tell of good blood and careful training. He is a good conversationalist, talks freely of his travels, knows much of music, is exceptionally well-read on matters of [the] moment and is a close student of affairs in general.

Loveland's friendship and society connections aside, Henwood was often too brash for his newfound acquaintances. Some of the women he met in Denver's leisure society found him overbearing and controlling. One said of him, "He was the sort of man who quarreled with waiters in cafes. If things didn't exactly suit he raised a fuss about them and sent them back, and argued with the waiter." Another remembered, "We might have our tastes and all that but it didn't make a bit of difference. If there was a certain kind of wine that Henwood liked, we must drink it—and like it, too."

He had a reputation as a brawler and troublemaker, particularly if he had been drinking. Before his arrival in Denver, he had taken the worst of it in a barroom fight with a total stranger in Seattle. In an odd way, the scars he gathered through the years, particularly one over his right eye and another, longer one just in front of his right ear, gave him an air of danger. In Denver, he flew into a fury one night over some slight at Tortoni's, a popular and upscale Arapahoe Street restaurant, and broke several chairs. He was bested in a fistfight with a chauffeur outside the Navarre, a fashionable bar, restaurant, and brothel on Tremont Place, opposite the Brown Palace. He was arrested at the Brown early one morning for banging on the door of a young actress to attract her attention.

Still, he managed to win the friendship and support of powerful Denverites. His business arrangement with John Springer quickly ripened into a friendship and the young promoter became a constant companion of the Springers. The spirited Isabel had no reservations about inviting Henwood to join their theater parties or to travel to the Springers' Cross Country Ranch.

Henwood lived what could be described charitably as a checkered life. Born in Italy in 1877 while his parents were vacationing there, he was the only son of Harold F. Henwood Sr., a prominent New Jersey businessman and philanthropist, who died only six months after Frank's birth. Young Henwood was well provided for. His father left him an estate of forty thousand dollars and, for a time, he received a thousand dollars a month for living expenses, which enabled him to travel the world as a gentleman vagabond.

As a young man, he drifted from town to town, trying his hand at various trades, including newsboy, piano salesman, motion-picture promoter, and real-estate seller. At various times, he lived in New York City, Memphis, Seattle, Alaska, British Columbia, Saskatchewan, Boston, Montreal, Toronto, San Francisco, Los Angeles, and Australia. He rested frequently, to recover his health. Henwood suffered from poor physical health much of his life. He frequently went long periods without employment and was hospitalized on several occasions for unspecified ailments. Mental instability was suggested by his frequent scrapes over women and his propensity for barroom brawls.

❖

Following Henwood's conviction in 1911 for second-degree murder, John Bottom set about heading off his client's being sent to the state penitentiary at Cañon City for the rest of his life with a series of simultaneous legal maneuvers.

John T. Bottom. (Courtesy of the Denver Public Library, Western History Department)

Judge Greeley Whitford had set July 5, a week after a jury ruled him guilty of killing George Copeland, as the date to begin the legal process of trying Henwood for the murder of von Phul. Bottom argued that the killings were one act, not two, and "that one conviction is all that can be had." District Attorney Willis V. Elliott, too, found little joy in Henwood's conviction because he had been sure the jury would return a verdict of murder in the first degree. He was reluctant to see Henwood go to trial for shooting von Phul because if a jury found Henwood not guilty, based on his claim of self-defense, it would invalidate the verdict in the Copeland case. If, the reasoning went, Henwood were not guilty of the murder of von Phul, he would also be not guilty of killing Copeland, leaving the state with no convictions. Henwood would go free.

On July 7, Bottom filed a plea of former jeopardy in Denver District Court, based on his previous claim that the two slayings were, in fact, one act and Henwood therefore could not be tried a second time. It fell to Judge Whitford to determine whether the shots fired by Henwood constituted a single act even though two people were killed. He was in no hurry to step into the controversy, citing a crowded court docket to postpone the hearing indefinitely. At the same time, Bottom began the long process of appealing the Copeland conviction to the Colorado Supreme Court. In his motion, he charged ninety-one errors in the trial.

While the appeals dragged on, Henwood continued to pass his life in the County Jail, where he had come to live fairly comfortably. As comfortably as one could in a steel cage. Reporters enjoyed extraordinary access to him. In July 1911, *The Post's* Louise Engel Scher visited Henwood's jail "home" and found him in a talkative mood, about everything but his trials and his family.

Scher asked Henwood about his childhood and his mother. "Let's not talk about her. She's dead." His eyes, she wrote, teared up and he ran his hand through his hair and said, impatiently, "Why should my people interest the public?" He was less shy about Cora Carpenter and Thomas Lepper, the two Springer servants who, he said, had lied against him in his first trial. He praised John Springer, "a good man, a kind man…the one man who stuck by me, encouraged me and helped me with my company." He vowed that when freed, "I'm going to stay right here in Denver and face this thing out. Surely, anyone who is just will know that I did this thing in self-defense, as Mrs. Springer told me three times the afternoon of the shooting that Mr. von Phul had threatened to kill me." He had become adept at using the newspapers to present his case to the public.

As summer evolved to winter, Henwood was no closer to freedom. Despite the delays, he remained upbeat. He began work on a dogsled in the jail workshop because he planned an expedition to Alaska, a place he read about extensively and was fond of, after his release. His moods continued to swing wildly and some feared for his sanity. In February 1912, he got drunk and initiated a fight with guard Isaac Goldman because Goldman refused to let him use the telephone in the jail office, one of the privileges Henwood had grown accustomed to.

The prosecution and the defense swapped legal arguments through the summer of 1912. On February 3, 1913, the state Supreme Court, ignoring most of Bottom's laundry list of complaints about the trial, agreed with him on a key point: Judge Whitford was wrong when he told the jury that there could be no manslaughter in the case. In its decision to reverse the verdict and grant Henwood a new trial, the judges referred to state law,

> These statutory provisions are a recognition of the frailty of human nature, the purpose of which is to reduce a homicide committed in the circumstances therein contemplated to the grade of manslaughter, either voluntary or involuntary, as the facts may warrant. It appears from the statutes that the unlawful killing of a human being, without malice and deliberation upon a sudden heat of passion, caused by a provocation apparently sufficient to excite an irresistible passion in a reasonable person, constitutes manslaughter.

The court's decision went on to say that "the evidence shows without question that von Phul knocked the defendant down with his fist by a blow so violent that [the] defendant struck the floor with great force. But if Henwood shot without taking into consideration the presence of others in the barroom, the court holds that he was not guiltless. But with the question of manslaughter taken from the jury, there was nothing left for the jury to do but find [the] defendant guilty of murder. They were thus deprived of their exclusive province to determine the grade of the offense from the evidence in the case."

Henwood waited nervously in the County Jail for the court's decision. He paced and puffed on his pipe. The phone rang. Jailer Jack Hardy called Henwood to the phone.

"Hello, this you, Henwood?" asked Bottom. "This is Mr. Bottom. Your case has been reversed and remanded."

A joyous expression on his face, Henwood turned to Hardy. "I've got a new trial!" He slammed the receiver down and began to dance about the room. "I knew it was coming! I knew it was coming! I have waited for it every day of my twenty-two months imprisonment. I am confident that I will be freed. My first trial was a farce." Prisoners throughout the jail cheered his good news as Henwood vigorously shook hands with those near him. His mood grew somber when one of the assembled reporters asked, "Will Mrs. Springer testify in your favor?" "I do not know where she is," he said, dodging the question. "I have heard nothing at all from her since my trial. No, I have never written to her."

Bottom next appealed to have the von Phul charges dropped because, under Colorado law, if a defendant is not tried within three terms of the sitting court, the charges become invalid. His strategy of delays and repeated appeals worked. On February 24, 1913, Judge Charles C. Butler agreed, ruling that Henwood should be set "at liberty," a vague bit of legalese that made it unclear whether he should be let out of jail or merely no longer held liable for the charge. One minute after Judge Butler handed down his decision, new District Attorney John A. Rush, elected the previous fall, refiled the murder charge in the von Phul matter. News of the dismissal barely caused a ripple in the local press. The assassinations of deposed Mexican president Francisco Madero and vice president José Maria Pino Suarez dominated the city's papers. The reversal of Henwood's fortunes was buried on page seven of *The Denver Republican*. He was no longer front-page news.

Sensing that he might succeed in freeing Henwood altogether, Bottom asked the court to release Henwood on both the Copeland and von Phul charges, claiming that since the charge of killing von Phul had been dismissed, putting him on trial again in the Copeland killing would constitute double jeopardy.

Judge Butler took up the matter in March. *The Post* already had made up its mind. In a page-one editorial, the newspaper, whose attorney, Bottom, was also the lead attorney for Henwood, proclaimed, "If Harold Henwood, who shot and killed Sylvester von Phul and George Copeland in Denver in May 1911, is allowed to go free by the courts on some technicality it will be to the lasting disgrace and dishonor of Colorado." It concluded, "Henwood must and will be punished. We have not reached such a pass in this state—and by God's mercy we never will—when a mere official technicality can give to such a man as Henwood immunity for the deliberate killing of two defenseless citizens."

Judge Butler heard arguments for a week. It was a text-book lesson in microscopic legal fine points. Both sides cited numerous cases and authorities. Henwood took so little interest in the arguments, he nodded off several times during the hearings.

Rush and Bottom argued vehemently. Rush accused Bottom of failing to prepare for the von Phul case, charging that he had never brought his witnesses to Denver for the trial. Bottom responded by putting himself on the stand, where he was forced to admit that he had not called any wit-nesses, but denied that he ever asked for a delay in starting the trial. John Chiles, assistant district attorney under Elliott, took the stand and said that it was Bottom, not the prosecu-tion, who requested the delay in the von Phul trial. Bottom was furious. "I did not ask the district attorney, or any of his men, to put the case over." He called on Henwood, and asked if he had ever heard Bottom ask for a delay. Henwood swore he hadn't. Then Rush took over, pressing Henwood to reveal the names of the witnesses whose expenses he had paid so they could come to Denver and testify on his behalf.

Rush: Who were these witnesses?

Henwood: I refuse to answer.

Bottom: You may answer.

Henwood: I positively refuse.

Rush: I ask that the court order the witness to answer the question.

Judge Butler: You must answer the question, Mr. Henwood. Your attorney advises it.

Henwood said nothing.

Judge Butler: You may write the names of the witnesses on a piece of paper and hand it to the district attorney, if you do not care to make their names public.

Henwood hesitated, then complied with the judge's suggestion.

Rush and Bottom weren't through. Bottom asked, loudly, of Rush, "Are you questioning my veracity?" "I certainly am," Rush retorted. Everyone began to shout. Judge Butler had heard all he wanted to. "I don't think all this matter is necessary, gentlemen. Let us get down to business."

The road to avoiding another trial in the Copeland death was rapidly becoming more slippery for Henwood. On March 29, Judge Butler affirmed his previous decision not to free Henwood, saying that while he dismissed the von Phul charge on a technicality, "the question of Henwood's innocence was not considered." He also censured the late district attorney, Willis Elliott, who conducted the state's case against Henwood in the first Copeland trial. "As soon as I came over to this court, I became aware that very loose methods had long prevailed in the work of the court clerk and the former district attorney, especially the latter. I was never so struck with the looseness of that system as I have been today. There are no adequate records of some of the transactions in this Henwood case under the former district attorney." He ordered Henwood to face a second trial for killing Copeland, beginning on May 28, 1913.

❖

Two years in jail since his arrest the night of the shooting and a bitterly fought trial that ended in his conviction had taken its toll on the salesman and promoter. Henwood's handsome features had grown sallow, his eyes sadder, his slicked-back hair thinner until he was nearly bald. Frances Wayne, who closely followed Henwood for *The Post*, remarked on the day he appeared for his second trial, "Every trace of color has gone from Henwood's face. The short, crinkled nose is pinched and waxy; the pouting, girlish lips have a purple tinge which when they part, show white gums and teeth made yellow by comparison.

"The eyes of this man, long imprisoned and overanxious, are sunk in their sockets and circled by heavy shadows. His appearance is ghastly, uncanny." Henwood experienced frequent periods of depression, and his well-known temper flared from time to time, leading to confrontations with guards and other prisoners.

He did not lack creature comforts in his cell. Unlike other prisoners, housed two to a cell, Henwood lived alone. His steel-walled cell was on what was known formally as "the lower west tier" and informally as "Millionaire's Row" or "Banker's Row," isolated from the clanging and banging of cell doors and the comings and goings of other prisoners and their visitors. Behind intersecting bars, which formed rectangles floor to ceiling, Henwood outfitted his small space with humble furnishings—pictures, books, and knick-knacks. Among his family photographs was one of his fifteen-year-old daughter, Frances, who wrote to him often. "To the right and across the wall extended over a regulation jail couch bed, is a pine board shelf," observed *Post* reporter James R. Noland, who made frequent visits. "It is loaded with books and various articles, including bottles of medicine, tobacco jars, a pipe or so, an alarm clock, two or three family portraits, the portrait of a former friend in the social world and many magazines."

Friends, men and women, were allowed to visit night and day. They brought him gifts, including boxes of cigars, bottles of wine and liquor. In the early days, flowers from female admirers were delivered frequently. As time wore on, however, visitors became fewer, and Henwood relied more on his own amusements. Reading became a passion. He particularly favored Arctic adventures. Titles on his primitive bookshelf included *Marchward Over the Ice*, *The Arctic Prairies*, and *The Grizzly Bear*. He often stayed up until three or four in the morning, reading about places he would never visit, and often slept until noon.

At 10 A.M. on May 28, Henwood's quest for freedom started over, with Judge Butler presiding. Attorneys lined up on the prosecutors' side of the large table before the judge were District Attorney Rush and two of his deputies, Harry N. Sales

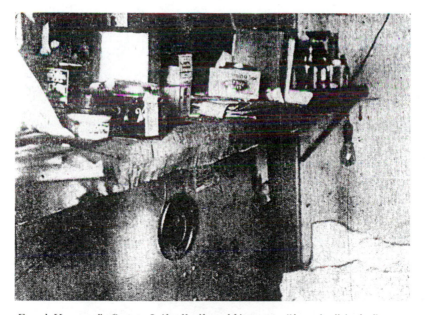

*Frank Henwood's County Jail cell allowed him many "luxuries," including two homemade shelves that held cigars, photographs, and gifts from admirers. (*The Denver Post, *May 28, 1913. Courtesy of the Colorado Historical Society)*

and Charles T. Mahoney. Seated across the large table from them, in the custom of trials of the day, were defense attorneys John T. Bottom, Judge O. N. Hilton, and Henry Lubers, former speaker of the state House of Representatives.

Henwood was on trial a second time, not for killing Tony von Phul, his rival for the attentions of Isabel Patterson Springer, but for the death of Copeland, an unsuspecting bystander. Judge Butler, who had a reputation as a letter-of-the-law jurist, was certain to adhere to the Colorado Revised Statutes, which provided that "all murder which shall be perpetrated...by any act greatly dangerous to the lives of others...shall be deemed murder in the first degree." Self-defense was virtually ruled out.

Jury selection was an aggravating, slow-moving process. Publicity in the 1911 trial and anticipation of the retrial made it difficult to find any man who hadn't formed an opinion on Henwood's guilt or innocence. The courtroom was crowded, potential jurors on one side, "men and women, boys and young girls who are always on the lookout for the erotic and sensational" jammed into the few chairs on the other.

The building of a jury dragged on for a week as dozens of prospective jurors were questioned and rejected by one side or the other. Eight men were selected fairly quickly, but the remaining four represented a series of stumbling blocks.

As days ground into a week, prosecutor Rush, adept at bending the newspapers to his purposes, vented his frustration to reporters. "I want to get a jury and have this case started," he grumped. "I'm tired of all this nonsense. The more the case is tried in the newspapers before it is tried in court the harder it will be to get a jury. Let us get down to the testimony in the case. I want to try the case in court and not in the newspapers." Quickly mollifying his audience of news gatherers, he said, "I don't blame the newspapers. There is hardly a man we may call as a juror who has not formed an opinion about the case."

Nearly two hundred men, in lots of one hundred, were called for the jury pool. The selection process was so tortuous that juror Thomas McAleer napped repeatedly. "Caressed by the tsetse bug," he was dismissed at the urging of Rush, causing the first of many clashes between defense attorney Hilton and the court. "Such an arbitrary use of discretionary power has never been recorded in the history of court trials," Hilton complained, perhaps overstating the case. "There is no law on the books which says a juror may not go to sleep and there is no evidence here, save the word of the district attorney, that the juror did go to sleep." Judge Butler responded curtly that he had seen McAleer drop into a prolonged slumber.

After eight days of wrangling, both sides were satisfied. The jury consisted in the main of young men, eight of them married. They were William F. Backes, automobile salesman; John T. Brattin, stenographer; John C. Brodie, cut-stone contractor; Timothy Calahan, creamery salesman; William T. Eccles, salesman; Adolph T. Hart, grocer; Marcus E. Johnson, accountant; George H. Layton, millwright; Charles McAllister, clerk; Harl Morton, clerk; Benjamin F. Slack, brass manufacturer; and William Seltzer Jr., broom manufacturer.

Though spectators continued to pack the courtroom, the number of curious men and women milling under the trees of the courthouse grounds was greatly diminished. The trial itself was, in large part, a rehash of the 1911 proceedings. Some witnesses, including the Springer family chauffeur Thomas Lepper, and Cora Carpenter, the housekeeper who claimed to have found Mrs. Springer's ripped nightgown after Henwood's all-night visitation, could not be located. Carpenter's testimony from the 1911 trial was read into the record.

The most effective witness for the prosecution was a man unable to appear at the first trial, Colorado Springs businessman James W. Atkinson, whose left leg was shattered by one of Henwood's bullets, leaving him permanently unable to walk unaided. In one of the more bizarre moments of the trial, the bulky Atkinson entered the courtroom on crutches and, as he paused at the doorway, a flash of lightning lit the room and a tremendous clap of thunder shook the building. Clad in a white suit, his pale skin and white hair gave him the appearance of a specter. His gigantic figure seemed to fill the doorway.

Assisted by several men, Atkinson hobbled to the witness chair as the jury watched closely. Once seated, he looked directly at the jury, never giving Henwood the briefest glance. Henwood stared into the tabletop in front of him, content to make notes, as he often did, with a little black pencil. The jury listened raptly as Atkinson described what he saw the night of the murder.

> I saw Henwood put his hand under von Phul's face. He said something I didn't hear. Almost immediately afterward von Phul struck him. There was a man in the way and I didn't see the blow, but heard it hit his face. Henwood fell down, first on his hips and then full length on the floor. As soon as he fell I said to Copeland, "Let's get out, there's going to be a fight." Henwood put one hand on the floor and started to rise, reaching for his hip pocket. He came to a standing position and then pulled his gun. One or two men attempted to grab hold but he shook them off and fired.

Questioned by Rush as to von Phul's position at the time, Atkinson didn't hesitate. "He had turned back to the bar with his right hand resting on it." In short, von Phul never assumed the threatening position Henwood claimed. It was a crushing blow to the defense's case.

Atkinson told how he had been struck by one of Henwood's shots. "I was five or six feet from the bar when I was hit. I took one or two steps. My leg hurt and I went down. I hopped a couple of times and said, 'My God! I'm shot!' By

*James W. Atkinson, assisted into court to testify. (*The Denver Times, *June 7, 1913. Courtesy of the Colorado Historical Society)*

that time everybody was out of the bar except Henwood. He picked up his straw hat and then came over to me.

"He said, 'I shot you?'"

"I said, 'Yes, you did.'"

"He said, 'Can I help you?'"

"I said, 'No, you've done enough for me already. Get out and leave me alone.'"

❖❖❖

On June 9, the tension that had been simmering between the two teams of lawyers since the trial began burst into the open. Henwood attorney Lubers, who remained in the background through the early days of the trial, asked Judge Butler if he would excuse the jury so he could call attention to a statement credited to the district attorney in the previous day's newspaper. After the jury left the room, Lubers raised a copy of *The Post* overhead and said, "As your honor perhaps knows, it will be necessary for the defense to produce evidence that von Phul had made threats against the life of Harold F. Henwood, the defendant. And where else can we seek those witnesses except in the environment wherein they live?" Lubers's allusion was to two prostitutes, Katherine Clark and Gladys Parker, who worked at Verona Baldwin's house at 2020 Market Street and were willing to testify that they heard von Phul, whom they knew only as Tony, make threats against Henwood.

"It seems to the attorneys for the defense," Lubers continued, "that Mr. Rush, knowing this, willfully sought to intimidate those witnesses and frighten them from the stand by giving this purported interview, which was published in *The Post* of yesterday." Gripping the paper tightly, he read a quote by Rush, "'The statement has been made that women of the underworld will be put on the witness stand to bolster up the defense, and that a number of new witnesses will be sprung. If these witnesses are all right they, of course, have a right to testify, but I will not stand for a repetition of the Gertrude Patterson case [the 1910 murder trial in which a last-minute witness won Mrs. Patterson her freedom]. The grand jury is in session and any attempt of that kind will be quickly met.'"

"That, your honor," shouted Lubers, "seems to me to be nothing more than a deliberate attempt to intimidate witnesses for the defense. The office of the district attorney is the most powerful in the state, and we object to it using its power in such a manner as to drive our witnesses away, to frighten them. We want the court to admonish the district attorney to stop interviews." Rush squirmed in his chair but said nothing. (The two women did testify two days later, although they were discredited by the prosecution, which implied that they had been put up to it by a Wyoming madam. Rush hinted, strongly, that the madam and Henwood were frequent companions in his cell.)

No sooner did Lubers fall silent than Bottom rose to the attack. "And that's not all! I charge that the district attorney has been calling up men who have been favorable to the defense and warning them away from seeking to aid the defense in the finding of certain witnesses. I want it stopped. I…"

Rush could stand no more. Leaping to his feet, he said, "That's not true! Name one!"

"Felix O'Neill!" Bottom responded. "You called him up and told him to stop working in the interests of Henwood. You told him that if he knew of any evidence he should be helping the district attorney's office by concealing…"

"That's an untruth!"

"And you called up a newly appointed constable and told him to stop helping Henwood—and he had helped him before he had been appointed a constable."

"Yes," Lubers chimed in, "and you've been giving out the letters of Mrs. Springer every day to certain newspapers, trying to bolster up your own case!"

Rush, waving his arms wildly, shot back. "That's an untruth, an untruth, an untruth!"

"Prove it," said Lubers.

Before Rush could answer, Bottom renewed his attack. "And what's more, I hereby charge that John A. Rush, the district attorney, inspired another article, printed some time ago [on page one on March 10, 1913, which, among other things, proclaimed, "Henwood must and will be punished"] in *The Post* and headlined 'Thou Shalt Not Kill!'"

"That's not the truth," said Rush, when he could get a word in.

Bottom was furious. "Your honor. If John Rush charges me again with telling an untruth, I'm going to fight him, and fight him right in this courtroom!"

"Any place you say," seethed the district attorney.

The audience burst into loud laughter, causing Judge Butler to bang his gavel repeatedly and shout, "Gentlemen! Gentlemen!"

Chastened, the two attorneys debated, briefly, the merits of each other's witnesses and the punishment for perjury and intimidation of witnesses.

Growing angry, Bottom thundered, "He is a liar! He is a scoundrel!" Bottom swept the room with his arm and concluded, "He is unworthy to be considered as a man among men!"

The judge's gavel crashed down time after time, and he again admonished the attorneys, "Gentlemen! Gentlemen!"

Finally, the judge, who gave both sides, particularly the defense, great latitude in presenting their cases, even allowing Henwood to ramble at length about his motives, could stand no more. After a long silence while the feuding counsels stared at each other, he said, "We are engaged in the trial of a case, the most serious known to law, wherein the penalty may be death. Therefore we should be most careful. There was a time when there was only one tribunal, the court. Now, it seems, there are two. Lately it has become popular with lawyers to seek to influence the public through the newspapers and, at some later time, take their case to court. It seems that the attorneys have deemed it necessary to try this case in the newspapers. Efforts have been made by both sides to educate the public.

"It was unfortunate that [Rush's] interview was granted. While his motives, I am sure, were of the highest, his interview might be construed by these witnesses as a threat—and it is therefore unfortunate. Therefore, the court would ask that in the future, the attorneys for both sides refrain from such interviews and confine themselves to trying this case in the good, old-fashioned way—through sworn witnesses on the witness stand."

With the judge's admonition out of the way, Henwood took the stand in his defense and told basically the same story he told in the first trial, that he feared for his life because of repeated threats made, directly and indirectly, by von Phul. As Henwood retold his tale, he wandered around the courtroom, even resting his hands on the jury box railing

*Charles C. Butler, the judge at the second Frank Henwood trial. (*The Denver Post, *June 24, 1928. Courtesy of the Colorado Historical Society)*

and addressing the jurors. He reiterated that his relationship with Mrs. Springer was strictly platonic. He never, he swore, tore her nightgown. And he came back to the reason he fired the shots. "Because I was in fear of my life, because of threats, because of the attitude of that man, his brutality, his size—he was of powerful, athletic frame—everything tended to give me the idea he was going to take my life."

Four days after his outburst at the attorneys for both sides, Judge Butler revisited the issue. First, he excused the jury. Leaning forward on the edge of his seat, he began a most extraordinary oration, one not seen previously in the West Side Court, where lawyerly free-for-alls and histrionics were the norm.

"I have something to say to counsel now present and to all lawyers practicing before this bar as to the conduct of cases. The practice in this court is of a solemn nature, since in many instances the charges are so grave, the penalties so far-reaching. That a jury may arrive at a just estimate of the evidence and thus render a fair verdict between the defendant and the people, every means should be put forth to attain the facts in a calm, dispassionate way.

"There are various ways of examining witnesses. There is one method employed by attorneys today—the vigorous method. Sometimes in their zeal counsel approach the witness with voice raised, hands shaking, arms upraised and rush questions at him which tear him to pieces.

"Hereafter, I will not tolerate in this court that form of examination. Here there shall be no third degree. An examination of witnesses by counsel is supposed to be an intellectual contest, with the odds always against the witness. Any tendency hence forth to bulldoze or intimidate or terrorize witnesses will be checked and the court will order the immediate imprisonment and fine of any attorney who continues this way.

"Anything of a vaudeville nature, anything calculated solely to amuse the audience will immediately be checked by the officers of this court. Mr. Bailiff, call the jury."

In the days that followed, many of the same witnesses were called and recounted information they gave in the 1911 trial. One witness was notably absent—Isabel Patterson Springer. Now living in the East, she was reported at various times to be on her way to Denver or hiding in Colorado or traveling in South Africa or Europe or living in Chicago or New York City.

Bottom felt certain that Isabel, whose appearance on the stand two years earlier had done nothing to support Henwood's case, could convince this jury that Henwood had acted honorably. The prosecution was not about to let that happen. In a brilliant stroke, Rush used newspaper interviews to warn that if Isabel returned to Denver and changed even a comma of her testimony she would be arrested for perjury. In addition, it was made clear that if she took the stand on Henwood's behalf, all her "foolish little letters" would be put before the public's prying eyes. "They will prove the degeneracy of three people, and prove it conclusively," said Rush. Over the objections of the defense, Mrs. Springer's testimony from the 1911 trial, the one in which she had given little support to Henwood, was read into the record.

On June 14, seventeen days after the second trial began, Judge Butler called the attorneys together to discuss his instructions to the jury on possible verdicts. They spent until six that afternoon going over what each side wanted to be included—first- and second-degree murder, voluntary and involuntary manslaughter, or acquittal. Self-defense was not an option, though Bottom and Lubers argued vigorously for it to be included. *The Denver Times*, adding a bit of humor to the discussion and perhaps still chafing under the judge's complaint that the case was being tried in the newspapers, was of the opinion that "Judge Butler's impression from the discussion was that the instructions—to suit all the attorneys—would read about this way:

1. The defendant is guilty.
2. The defendant is not guilty.
3. The defendant is neither guilty nor innocent.
4. The costs of this case shall be assessed against the newspaper reporters, to be paid out of their salaries at the rate of $100 a week.

Attorneys for both sides assured the judge that they were coming to the end of their long lists of witnesses waiting to appear. But Bottom and his assistants had one more surprise. They unleashed it the next day when John Springer, the wronged husband and Henwood's onetime business partner, took the stand on Henwood's behalf.

Chapter Ten
AN OLD FRIEND: "ALWAYS A GENTLEMAN"

WHEN JOHN SPRINGER mounted the witness stand to testify on June 15, 1913, he was no longer the energetic, highly political club man who had become a well-known figure in Denver. His political career and his reputation as a bachelor and an escort of beautiful women behind him, Springer looked older than his fifty-three years, despite his natty clothing. His face had grown paunchy, his eyes appeared tired, and he was nearly bald. The strain on him since the shooting at the Brown Palace and the subsequent scandal weighed him down.

That he testified for Henwood was an astonishing turn of events because he had remained aloof from the entire affair. When his wife's tangled relations with Tony von Phul and Frank Henwood came to light, Springer distanced himself from the case, and from her. "Mrs. Springer made mistakes," he told a reporter in 1911. "But why should I, as the head of one of the largest institutions in the city, be brought into this unfortunate affair? If Mrs. Springer has sinned, she alone must answer for those sins."

Except to deny emphatically that he had filed for a divorce (which he had), he remained mum during the very public settlement negotiations with his wife that were carried on in the city's daily newspapers. "I say to you as I have said to all others who have asked me to make a statement—that I positively refuse to be interviewed. I can't see why this affair should be kept up."

Not only had he declined to testify at Henwood's first trial, he didn't attend any of the sessions at the West Side courtrooms between June 19 and 29, 1911, preferring to conduct business as president of the Continental Trust Company and to manage his horse and cattle ranch. Yet, two years later, he strode confidently into Judge Butler's court, convinced at last in his mind that Henwood had acted on his behalf against von Phul and prepared to present his former business associate as a paragon of civil behavior.

He entered the packed courtroom the picture of up-to-date fashion. "Mr. Springer [was] smartly dressed, self contained," noted *The Post*. "He wore a spring suit of soft gray wool, his red-socked feet were encased in white oxfords—latest, flat-heeled model—a red tie was held by a dreamy pearl in front of the high, chokey collar. In one nervous hand Springer twirled a cane and in the other held a pair of buff-colored suede gloves."

Seated a few feet away at the defendant's table, Henwood kept a close eye on the man whom he considered one of his closest friends in Denver, though they had not spoken to each other in more than two years. Henwood didn't look well, and, in fact, had been suffering from a cold, the result of his habit of keeping his cell window open wide winter and summer. He leaned toward his attorney and said softly, "For two years I've waited for this." He sat back and listened.

Defense attorney O. N. Hilton began quizzing Springer on his views about the relationship between Henwood and the former Mrs. Springer:

Question: Did the defendant at any time, on any occasion, treat Mrs. Springer with impropriety?

Answer: He did not.

Q: Had Henwood been your guest before?

A: Yes.

Q: What had been his course of conduct as far as it came to your attention, on each and every occasion, to Mrs. Springer, your then wife?

John W. Springer testifying that Frank Henwood always acted the gentleman around Isabel. (The Denver Republican, *June 17, 1913. Courtesy of the Colorado Historical Society)*

A: Mr. Henwood always was a gentleman.

At that moment, a young woman in the audience clapped her hands. She was ejected from the courtroom.

During his time on the witness stand, Springer pointed out that he, his wife, and Henwood often met socially, at their home on Washington Street and "at the Brown Palace Hotel, at the theater, at the bank, at the ranch and at many other places."

His testimony complete, Springer was excused. In one of the most riveting moments of the trial, he walked immediately to Henwood, put his left hand on the prisoner's shoulder, and extended his right hand. "Hello, Frank. How are you, old fellow?" he said with a smile. For a fleeting second, Henwood appeared to lose his composure, his eyes tearing up, then he rose and took Springer's hand. "Pretty well, thank you, John. And thank you, John."

Everything Springer told the jury reinforced Henwood's claims that he was acting only as the older man's friend, to spare him the embarrassment of a court case about the conduct of his wife with von Phul. For Henwood, the public reuniting of the two men came two years too late. If it had taken place in the 1911 trial, the outcome almost certainly would have been different.

Prosecutor Rush wasted no time heaping scorn on Springer's courtroom declarations. He agreed that Springer's testimony about Henwood's gentlemanly behavior toward Isabel was correct "within the witness's knowledge."

The last of the witnesses was heard on June 17. All that remained before the jury began its deliberations were Judge Butler's instructions to the jury and closing arguments by both sides. Despite the drawn-out trial, Henwood continued to believe that he would be set free. "I think I have a good chance of being acquitted," he told *The Denver Republican*. "I have looked at the case from every angle, and while I realize there is damaging testimony against me, I believe we have it offset by testimony offered by the defense.

"I have not worried as much over the outcome of this trial as I did over the last for I am getting a squarer deal all 'round. The prosecuting attorney is a bit more offensive in this trial than was District Attorney Elliott, but Judge Butler is very much fairer than was Judge Whitford, before whom I was tried before."

As the day's business began, Judge Butler carefully explained its options to members of the jury. He instructed them that if they found Henwood guilty they must state in their verdict whether they find him guilty of first- or second-degree murder, or of voluntary or involuntary manslaughter. In the case of first-degree murder, he added, they must fix the penalty of death or life imprisonment. Self-defense was not mentioned.

At 10:40 A.M., the doors to the courtroom were thrown open and a large crowd, as many as five hundred people, began forcing its way inside, tearing a screen door off its hinges. The room filled quickly with spectators, and many were left outside as the closing arguments began.

❖

Prosecutor Charles Mahoney spoke first, and held nothing back, attacking not only the "cowardly" shooting but Henwood's character. "Two men are now in their graves and one is crippled for life as a result of Henwood's cowardly act. And it was a cowardly act, for he shot Sylvester von Phul in the back. Henwood, the man who fired those cowardly shots into von Phul's back, lived off of John Springer and his wife.

"He has never sat in the prisoner's dock," Mahoney noted, attempting to show that Henwood was given special treatment throughout his time in court. He was entirely right. Unlike most prisoners, confined to a chair in a small enclosure, Henwood was allowed to sit between his lawyers at the counselors' table and even allowed to wander around the courtroom. He often stood near the open windows to get relief from the stuffy air.

"Sometimes the heart of the prosecutor goes out to some of those poor wretches who have no breeding, no friends and no money to defend their cases. But we have no sympathy for this man, well educated and cultured, who tells us of the strength of his powerful eye and then fires cowardly shots into this man's back." He talked scornfully of Henwood's "commanding presence. He used this presence to strike a good side of von Phul, as he claimed. And he did strike a good side—with a .38 caliber bullet." Springer's last-minute and cordial testimony on behalf of Henwood, followed by a warm handshake in full view of the jury, was treated with scorn. "That incident, gentlemen of the jury, was an insult to your intelligence."

As he neared the end of his forty-minute summation, Mahoney took von Phul's bloodied brown-checked coat in his hands and held it up before the jury. The prosecutor tore into Henwood's story that he acted in self-defense. "If Henwood thought von Phul was a dangerous man, why did he follow him up, and follow him up, and follow him up? I say that Henwood provoked that quarrel in the barroom of the Brown Palace Hotel so that he might murder him. I say that he was the aggressor in this quarrel. And yet this defendant attempts to make the plea of self-defense!

"I have to say this, that Henwood provoked this quarrel, that he shot von Phul in the back, that he shot at him and kept on shooting, even after von Phul had gone behind other men; but just the same, Henwood kept on shooting, and in doing so he shot George E. Copeland and sent him to his grave; and this, I say, was murder in the first degree."

Defense attorney Lubers followed and focused immediately on the prosecution's attitude toward his client. "I knew they were going to ask for a verdict of murder in the first degree. I knew it from the vindictiveness and malice they extended from the time that the first juror was called to the box until the last witness in rebuttal had been examined. They must have another notch in their pistol. Henwood's life must be delivered to them, in spite of all the evidence that has been adduced at this trial."

Judge Charles Butler chastised opposing attorneys John Bottom and John Rush for intimidating witnesses and warned both men to use restraint. (The Denver Post, *June 13, 1913. Courtesy of the Colorado Historical Society)*

Lubers, too, put von Phul's coat before the jury, arguing that the pattern of the bullet holes could be made only by the dead man reaching for his hip pocket and a revolver. Springer's testimony, he said, "was a vindication for Henwood—a real vindication. It showed that he was not a breaker of homes, but a protector of homes."

There was a five-minute recess, then Lubers, his powerful voice loud enough to be heard by those gathered on the lawns outside the courthouse, asked the jury's mercy. "We want you to give a verdict that you will not be sorry for, and remember that if there is a verdict against this defense you must give it with your eyes before God Almighty, and give it in such a way that when you pass before the Great Judge you may go there with a heart free and with the feeling that his guilt was absolutely beyond a reasonable doubt.

"But we ask you for a verdict of not guilty. He was protecting the home of a friend—and the final closing of this tragedy was all through fear of the malignant, hating von Phul."

Bottom, who had befriended Henwood and had been his legal counsel almost since the sound of the shooting died away in 1911, mounted a careful examination of the witnesses' testimony. But he also couldn't resist a last chance to attack his rival, John Rush, charging that the district attorney had "framed up" the evidence and "trained" the witnesses. "There is not one of you gentlemen of the jury who was not asked whether you would be influenced by pathos and dramatic action. He meant pathos and dramatic action on the part of the district attorney and the state's witnesses. Just remember the witness [von Phul's cousin Fred] Cooke and how he acted on the witness stand. Remember how [Rush] acted when he had Henwood on the witness stand; how he asked Gladys Parker whether she was not a common prostitute. John Rush reminds me of a catfish in the Missouri River in which I used to fish, and I want to say to him that he is on my hook."

Bottom appealed to the jury. "The shooting of Copeland was purely accidental." He, too, asked the jurors to examine von Phul's jacket and draw their own conclusions. Bottom had been speaking for almost three hours. All the participants clearly were anxious to finish, because after a brief recess, rather than adjourn for the day, prosecutor Rush began the last summation. The courtroom clock read 7:35 P.M. as Rush launched into a three-hour diatribe that savaged Henwood, whom he described as "a wanderer," "a vagabond," "a ne'er-do-well," and his behavior toward Mrs. Springer.

"What do we find this vagabond doing a week after he met Mrs. Springer? We find him calling her by the pet name of 'Sassy.' John W. Springer came into this courtroom and said that Harold F. Henwood always had acted the gentleman. I say no gentleman, and no husband who is a gentleman himself, would allow a stranger to come into his home and call his wife by a nickname a week after he had met her! How would you like your wife to go shopping and to theaters and for long automobile rides with a vagabond who had drifted into town and butted into your circle?"

Turning his attention to the lurid stories of nocturnal goings-on at the Springer ranch, when Henwood spent the night, his bedroom separated only by a bathroom from Isabel Springer's suite on the second floor, Rush's diatribe rolled on. "Springer wasn't there on this fatal night of the torn nightgown and the mussed up bed. Henwood's bed was untouched that night. Do you think he went out and sat on the woodpile all night? Or on the settee? No, the next morning Mrs. Springer's bed was mussed up and Henwood's untouched— and Mrs. Springer's nightgown was torn before and behind from the vigorous treatment it had received that night!"

He tugged at class prejudices, painting for a jury made up of working and, for the most part, married men a view of "high society" where misbehavior ran rampant. "Now, in high society, where morals are sunken to the lowest depths, where men don't care what people may do to their wives, that may be the definition of a gentleman. If so, God help us! And if it is so, it would be better to send this man to the penitentiary for life, or to stretch his neck until he is dead, rather than send him back to such an environment!" Rush was not satisfied excoriating Henwood. He took Springer to task, too. "What sort of a gentleman do you call a man who will stand by while another man performs the duties of a husband to his wife and, after he divorces this wife because she has allowed this man to perform those duties, comes in here and calls his rival a gentleman and takes his hand before the public?

"That's the sort of a gentleman John W. Springer is—but I'm sure he's not your kind of gentleman."

Shaking an accusing finger at the defendant, he shouted, "We have sunk low, indeed, when this society with its lax morals, its exchangeable wives, its indifferent husbands, its licentious ways, its preying lovers, its shameless women, is allowed to exist without let or hindrance!"

Weary jurors hoped he was coming to the end. But Rush had one more salvo. "Gentlemen of the jury, because this defendant loved the wife of another man and saw her slipping away from him he shot Tony von Phul in the back. Because of a simple assault and battery, he shot von Phul in the back. He shot him in the back out of hatred, out of revenge, and the verdict can be nothing but murder in the first degree. And, gentlemen, when you return your verdict I shall expect you to rid this community of this vermin which fastened itself on a home and ruined and degraded it. I shall expect you to bring in a verdict of murder in the first degree, with a penalty of death!"

At 10:30 P.M., he sat down. Twenty-two days after it began, it was done. The jury retired for the night. Each side believed it had convinced the jury of the righteousness of their case. Henwood was sure of it.

The next morning, members of the jury gathered in their conference room at 8:30 A.M. and began debating the verdict, but after six hours they hadn't reached a decision. All agreed on the first ballot that he was guilty, but only three wanted a first-degree murder decision; the other nine were split among verdicts ranging from second-degree murder to manslaughter.

At noon the jury broke for lunch and made its customary walk to the Home Dairy restaurant at Sixteenth and Welton Streets, then resumed its discussion at 2 P.M. Given permission to sit at a jail window where he could see into the second-story jury room of the courthouse fifty yards away, Henwood was buoyed by what he saw. He could see the jurors pacing back and forth, breaking into small groups and talking animatedly, sometimes breaking into laughter. "I think they're going to free me," he said to another prisoner. "Don't you think so?" There was no response. Henwood's hopes were high. "Men don't laugh when they're sending another to the penitentiary, or to the gallows."

An hour, then two, passed.

Suddenly, there was a buzz in the courthouse. After thirty ballots, the jury had reached its decision. The bailiff quickly called the downtown offices of Bottom and Rush to tell them to come to the courthouse. Deputies hurried to fetch Henwood at the jail. Judge Butler took his place. The jury, sequestered on the second floor, announced it was ready to report its verdict.

The deputies found Henwood in a positive mood. He was sure that the jury had heard his claim that he was acting only as Springer's friend, that he was deathly afraid of the volatile von Phul and had acted on those fears to defend himself.

Wearing a derby and a dark suit and vest and surrounded by deputy sheriffs John Ronaldson, William Arnett, and James Rinker and by John Kenney, who had succeeded Patrick Riordan as warden, Henwood strode confidently toward his fate. He entered the sheriff's office adjacent to the courtroom and waited to be called. Almost absentmindedly he began fumbling in his pocket, searching for his tobacco pouch and pipe. He laughed when he realized his pipe was missing.

"Guess I must have gotten excited when I left the jail building," he said to the lawmen. "I left my pipe behind."

"Have a cigarette," offered one of the guards.

He took one and said, politely, "Guess I'll have to ask for a match, too."

He glanced around the room while he waited. "Gee, I'm well protected. Let's see, how many deputies are there?" He counted six. "Well, I guess that's enough to keep me safe, isn't it?"

Someone said, "Worried, Frank?"

"Why should I be? They're going to acquit me. I feel sure of it."

Then it was time. "Frank," said Deputy Arnett, "they're coming down."

Henwood straightened, discarded his cigarette, stepped forward, and smiled. "All right, Billy."

Chapter Eleven
THE FINAL VERDICT: "I HAVE REGRETS"

JUDGE CHARLES C. BUTLER leaned forward. "Gentlemen, have you reached a verdict?"

"We have," said foreman George Layton. He handed a folded piece of paper to court clerk John Bergen, who passed it up to Judge Butler, who glanced at it and handed it back. "You will listen to the reading of your verdict, gentlemen."

Rain clouds gathered outside the courthouse. Light faded from the room, and it took on a dismal gray hue.

Bergen unfolded the note, read it carefully to himself, then read to the packed courtroom in a clear, loud voice. "State of Colorado, City and County of Denver. In the District Court. People of the State of Colorado vs. Harold Frank Henwood, defendant, No. 20182. We, the jury, find the defendant, Harold F. Henwood, guilty of murder in the first degree, as charged in the information herein and fix the penalty at death."

"Is that your verdict?" the clerk asked the jury. All twelve agreed that it was.

The large clock on the courtroom wall read 4:37. For a few seconds after the verdict was read, the ticking of the clock was the only sound to be heard. Henwood, Bottom, and Lubers sat, unmoving, ashen-faced. Gripping the arms of his chair, Henwood leaned over and whispered to Lubers, "Can I have the privilege of addressing the jury?"

"No, not now."

Suddenly, there was pandemonium as spectators and reporters who were jammed into the steamy courtroom bolted for the door to spread the news. Some rushed the defendant's side of the long table to the judge's left. Bottom and Lubers leaped to their feet and shouted, "Not this way! Not this way!" Bailiff George Kelly slammed his gavel on his desk and called for order. Those in the crowd paused, milled about for a moment, then retraced their steps to their seats. Judge Butler thanked members of the jury and dismissed them.

Henwood rose slowly to his feet, his legs barely able to support him. To no one in particular he said, softly, "I am not afraid of death." Deputies surrounded him to keep the crowd at bay while Henwood shook hands with his attorneys and with his friend Colorado Senator Thomas McCue, with whom he had had business dealings and who, for reasons known only to the senator, became Henwood's primary financial supporter. McCue sat in the courtroom through the twenty-two days of the trial.

Lawyers for both sides immediately began issuing self-serving interpretations on the verdict. Bottom was asked if the jury's decision marked the end of his attempts to have Henwood freed. He responded,

We haven't begun to fight. Henwood was wished on me by two of his young friends the morning after the shooting. The first time I saw him was in the City Jail. He told me his story and said, "If the names of my friends have to be dragged into this thing I'd rather plead guilty at the start and let them do what they please to me." That's not the language of a coward or craven, is it? From that moment I've believed in that boy. There are any number of grounds for an appeal. We'll find a way to carry on this case, never fear. For justice must be done the boy.

Prosecutor Rush told a reporter,

The sentimental public may regard me as cold blooded
and without warmth of heart. But I give you my word,
when I knew how the net was tightening about
Henwood as the days of the trial passed by, a great pity
for the man as a waster possessed me. When the jury
brought in that just verdict I wanted to cry—not
because I felt Henwood was getting what he did not
deserve, but because the man had made such a fool of
himself and had thrown away what should have been a
useful life. At the outset of the trial John W. Springer
came to me and asked that the thing be dropped or, if
that could not be, he urged me to leave the Springers
out of the trial. Mr. Bottom also made this appeal. I
answered that if the defense would leave the Springers
out, the prosecution was willing and anxious to make its
case on the events in the barroom. . . .

The jury heard and saw the witnesses, the jury
balanced the evidence, the judge was so anxious to be
fair that he leaned far to the side of the defendant and
made the prosecution work twice as hard as they otherwise would have had to work. The prosecution's part in
the trial of this case was clean as a hound's tooth.

The Denver Times, reflecting community outrage over a
series of trials in which alleged murderers had received light
sentences or had been turned loose, editorialized in favor of
the jury's death sentence:

This verdict clears the local atmosphere. The ancient
injunction, "Thou shalt not kill," had become a
byword in the mouths of the ignorant. Murderers had
gone unpunished of their crimes on flimsy pretext
and through false sentiment. Jurors had listened to

the galleries instead of to the law. Life had become quite cheap in this community. Last evening's verdict brings a return to sanity.

After the verdict, Henwood was shepherded by guards through more than a hundred curious bystanders, some of whom had lounged since morning on the lawns between the courthouse and the jail, and was taken to the condemned cell in the south upper wing on the second floor of the jail. He kept his eyes lowered, never glancing left or right.

Once in the condemned cell, Henwood would be kept under surveillance night and day so he couldn't take his life before the state could do it for him. Before he entered the cell, barren except for an iron cot and one chair, he was approached by warden John Kenney. "We must search you, Frank."

"All right, Johnnie."

As his clothes were removed, Henwood began shaking. Fearing that his nerves were giving way, a doctor was called and a small dose of strychnine prescribed. He refused it. When the search reached his vest, Henwood reached into one of the pockets and drew out a small piece of silver. "This is my last dime. I have been in jail just two years and am now at the end of my line. This goes and I am a broken man."

Also in the room were his attorneys and his friend Thomas McCue. Henwood told them, "The dying part I do not fear. It is the weeks I will spend here thinking that I have not been treated with fairness by some person, and prosecutor Rush, in particular. I look upon him as a persecutor, not as a prosecutor. He was malignant, vicious and unfair." He turned to McCue. "Dear old Tom. You have been the only daddy I ever had. You and John Bottom have stood by me, haven't you? If the law must have my life, it may have it. But it can't take your friendship, Tom, and dear old John Bottom's away from me, can it? I still have confidence in my friends on the outside."

*Frank Henwood leaving court after being found guilty of first-degree murder. (*The Denver Republican, *June 19, 1913. Courtesy of the Colorado Historical Society)*

Later, sitting on the bunk in his temporary home, he was alone except for guard Charles Boh, who perched on a chair outside the double set of bars that surrounded the six-by-six-foot cell. When dinner was announced, Henwood looked at Boh and said, "I can't eat, I'm so broken up." Boh nodded in sympathy. The condemned cell, the same one in which Giuseppe Alia, an Italian anarchist who murdered Father Francis Leo Heinrichs in St. Elizabeth's Catholic Church on February 23, 1908, had been housed, was a stark, depressing space. There were no rugs or curtains, as there were in Henwood's jail home for the past two years. Only steel. There were no privileges, although he was provided with reading materials and a typewriter. His lawyers would be his only visitors.

Asked again later if he wanted food, Henwood said, "No. Tell Johnnie [Kenney] I don't feel like eating. I would like to have my pipe and tobacco though." His well-used briar was brought to him. He packed and lit it, then walked to and fro in the small cell. His nerves were shot, and he couldn't stop

This previously unpublished photograph of Frank Henwood, center, with Deputy Sheriff W. W. Arnett, left, and an unidentified man was taken by Rocky Mountain News *photographer Harry Rhoads in 1913. (Courtesy of the Denver Public Library, Western History Department)*

pacing. He asked for Dr. C. B. James, the jail's doctor, who examined him and prescribed a one-thirtieth grain of strychnine as a stimulant to steady his heart. It wasn't until 2 A.M. that the condemned man lay down to sleep. As he lay on his bunk, he said to relief guard James Lalor, "Let's refrain from discussing the verdict."

He awoke at 5 A.M. but remained almost motionless. Lalor kept a close watch on him. At 7, a new guard, John Harding, came on duty. Harding and Lalor watched the prisoner in twelve-hour shifts. Henwood declined breakfast but asked for a cup of coffee, then another. Finally, he accepted lunch brought by Harding. He eagerly consumed a porterhouse steak, potatoes, coffee, and asparagus on toast, his favorite food, which he had become accustomed to during his relatively luxurious days as a privileged prisoner. Some comforts remained.

Despite the hearty meal, his mental health continued to decline. He told those around him that he was confident of acquittal in a third trial, but his demeanor had changed. He paced his cell for hours, his hands clasped behind his back. When guards asked questions, he responded with one-syllable answers. His despondency was deepening. Even frequent visits from evangelist Jim Goodheart and a Catholic priest, Father Panacelli, couldn't throw off his torpor.

Two days later, he was freed from his isolation on "murderer's row." The move into the general jail population was prompted by economics, not compassion. It was expensive having two guards watch him around the clock. Still, the switch buoyed Henwood's spirits. Other prisoners, mindful of the favors he had done them, welcomed him warmly. "There is certainly a difference between solitary confinement in a cell that has been occupied only by murderers and being locked up out here where you can see the sun," he told a reporter, then added quickly, "Not that I have any desire to be locked up at all, but that I feel almost like I had been given my liberty since being changed over here."

His first requests were for clean linen and a bath. It would be another month before he requested that his beard, which he had let grow during one of his depressed periods, be shaved off. Warden Kenney was taking no chances that Henwood, who vowed that he would never spend a day at the state penitentiary, would attempt suicide with a straight razor. For his shave, Henwood was escorted into a room and placed in a chair near the south windows. Kenney sat within two feet of Henwood, ready to leap if he tried to grab the razor as prisoner/barber Patsy Smith quickly shaved him without incident.

❖

For Harold Francis Henwood, two years and a wide social chasm lay between the comforts of the Brown Palace Hotel and the gray steel cell where he had become an erratic and, perhaps, mentally unbalanced recluse. A life filled with violent encounters and an inability to stay in one place for long pointed to a man with serious psychological problems. His moods in prison rose and fell, depending on the trends of his trials. Sometimes, he would lose control for no apparent reason.

A heavy black beard made him a stranger even to those who knew him. They might not have seen him anyway. As he worked, he always kept one eye on the main door to the jail. When he spied someone he knew, he scurried into his cell and remained there until they left. Warden John Kenney was instructed not to let anyone visit unless Henwood gave permission. He rarely gave it.

His routine never varied. Every morning at 6 o'clock, Henwood, a man for whom a roaming, will o' the wisp lifestyle was habit, diligently swept and mopped the corridor and cells in the federal wing of the jail. It was a decided change for him. After his 1911 conviction for second-degree murder, Henwood lived a comfortable life in his small cell. He paid extra to have his meals specially prepared by the jail's cook. Meals were sometimes delivered on fine china, accompanied by the proper silver, from the Brown Palace's kitchen. He wore his own clothes instead of prison-issue green-gray overalls. He was allowed to wander the hall outside his cell, and he received guests and telephone calls at all hours. He spent part of each day outside his cell rocking in a large rocking chair sent by a friend. It was rumored that he frequently was turned loose on Friday nights to visit the city's thriving houses "in which ladies of the evening cavorted and wine was consumed."

The steel walls of his cell were plastered with pictures of his favorite outdoor recreation, fishing. On one wall were two primitive bookshelves, one with an inkwell and a paste pot that allowed him to clip and paste into scrapbooks stories about him and his trials. Below the shelves was a small cupboard made from a packing case where he stashed gifts sent to him. His dark-blue suit and a new straw hat were hung carefully on a hanger. In one corner, a canary sang almost continually in its own prison.

After his funds ran out, he ate with other prisoners (a typical meal consisted of stew, black coffee, and bread without butter, all served on tin plates). He rarely saw friends and, most important, he began to understand that the chances of his life ending at the end of a hangman's noose were growing each day.

❖

Two days after the verdict was handed down, Bottom and Lubers began the appeals process again. The state was asked to spend twelve hundred dollars for transcripts in a paradoxical effort to save Henwood from the death sentence being carried out by the state. Henwood declared himself a pauper. His fiercest financial supporter, Senator McCue, perhaps sensing Henwood's hopes fading, was disinclined to continue bankrolling Henwood's fight for life, meaning the state would have to pick up the tab to have 600,000 pages of court documents transcribed. Bottom and Lubers told the court that none of Henwood's attorneys had ever been paid for their services, nor did they expect to be. Judge Butler put off a decision on the request until pending appeals had been decided.

Bottom's contention that errors in the trial gave Henwood a third chance at freedom drew support in the press from other attorneys. A general feeling against the death penalty was rising, and members of the Colorado State Federation of Women's Clubs were prepared to take the issue to the voters if Henwood failed to get a new trial. In the trial's aftermath, Mrs. Edward P. Costigan, the club's president—who, in a small touch of irony, lived around the corner from John Springer in Capitol Hill—expressed the disgust that many society women felt about the scandal and about Henwood's involvement in it. "While I am opposed to capital punishment and can't repress a shudder of horror at even the thought of life imprisonment, I think that a man of Henwood's stamp should suffer confinement for a long number of years. The thinking people have no illusions concerning Henwood's character and no false emotionalism concerning him."

Bottom plunged ahead with appeals. "More error exists in the record of this trial than in that of the first trial, the only difference being that the error this time was introduced by the district attorney and not by the court. I am more confident of a new trial this time than I was after the former trial." On June 28, Bottom petitioned Judge Butler for a third trial, citing twenty-seven errors committed in the course of the second trial, including the arrest of defense witness John T. Garver for perjury, the prosecution's intimidation of witnesses, and the district attorney's behavior, in court and in the newspapers. At the request of the district attorney's office, which claimed it had not received a copy of the motion, Judge Butler postponed the hearing.

Henwood's options and hopes were dwindling. On July 17, Judge Butler took up another of the condemned man's appeals, but Henwood seemed to have lost interest in the proceedings. He strode into court with his usual confident air, a smile on his face, but two years in jail had taken its toll. His weight was down considerably, and his face looked haggard and nearly devoid of color. He quietly took his place between Bottom and Lubers.

The judge allotted each side two-and-a-half hours to present its arguments. The hearing lasted most of two days. The animosity that boiled over between Bottom and Rush during the second trial flared again. Rush began by submitting twenty-one affidavits disputing Bottom's claims that members of the jury had expressed a desire to convict Henwood before the trial began. And he strongly defended his attitude in presenting the state's case. "The innuendoes and charges made in the motion for a new trial are wholly unsupported by the oath or affirmation of any person," he said, adding that he filed his affidavit merely out of an abundance of caution. It was a clear, if indirect, attack on Bottom, with whom he had clashed several times during the 1913 trial, leading both men to be admonished by the judge to mind their manners.

Bottom attacked Rush and his efforts "to poison the minds of the jury. What jury would acquit this defendant with the prosecutor's question, 'Is this another Patterson jury?' ringing in their ears? What right had he to say that Henwood was a home wrecker and that John W. Springer was his meal ticket?" He charged that Rush browbeat and "bully ragged" witnesses for the defense. He also asked that if an appeal were granted, that the trial be moved to another venue because it would be impossible to find jurors who had not made up their minds to Henwood's guilt or innocence.

Rush launched a vicious counterattack, insisting that he was right when he called Henwood "a vagabond, a nomad, a rover, a parasite, a vermin, a leech who had fastened himself upon John W. Springer." He added,

> If the district attorney paints the defendant as a perfect angel he will not be criticized, but if he tells the truth he is attacked as an outlaw, not only in the courtroom but also in the public press. Talk about conduct of the case! According to [the attorneys for the defense] it might be all right for them to come in here with perjured affidavits, mutilated or forged records and a coat, which upon the face of it, shows that it has been cut with a knife. And another thing, it was a dirty trick of defendant's counsel to have Springer walk down here and shake hands with the defendant. Talk about conduct of a case!

Rush accused Henwood's lawyers of, in effect, falling asleep during the trial. Lubers leaped to his feet to protest.

"Wait and see what I have to say," said Rush. "If you keep your ears open you might get something through your noodle." He pointed out that the judge declined to allow into the record many of his arguments. He also delivered something of an apology. "I confess that we attorneys, in our personal quarrels, acted like pickpockets and fishmongers [during the trial]."

Bottom's rebuttal focused on Rush's closing argument. He took particular offense to Rush's statement relating to Henwood's birth in Italy—that "while he may not be an Italian he has at least inherited the racial freedom with a stiletto." "The district attorney," said Bottom, "slanders a whole race of people in order to prejudice 12 men to convict Henwood." There were more charges and countercharges over bits and pieces of evidence that should, or should not, have been allowed into the trial. Judge Butler let both sides have their say.

The following Saturday was Henwood's sentencing hearing, and it began with Judge Butler's ruling on the request for a new trial. "During this argument I have wanted all to be said which could be said," Judge Butler said. "I did not wish to have anything withheld from me. The benefit of every reasonable doubt was given to the defendant, and every reasonable objection by his counsel was sustained. It seems to me that the defendant has had a fair trial. The motion for a new trial will be denied."

Henwood's face betrayed no emotion. He stared impassively at the district attorney, then looked toward the gallery, which was almost empty, an indication of how the public's interest in his case had waned since 1911. As the attorneys for both sides wrangled over a motion to stay the judgment, Henwood said to Bottom, "I'm going into the sheriff's office to telephone. If you want me, I will be in there." He strolled out of the courtroom, followed by an officer. He talked on the phone briefly, then stepped outside into a light rain and turned up his collar against the gloomy weather.

When Henwood reentered the courtroom, Judge Butler asked the defendant if he wanted to say anything. His face pale,

his lips dry, and his voice quaking, Henwood had to support himself on the edge of the prisoner's box as he read a statement:

> As God is my judge, I did not enter that barroom with
> murder in my heart. It is not in fear of the sentence
> that awaits me that I protest my innocence. I was
> shooting in fear of my life. For those lives I have taken,
> if this life of mine could bring them back God knows
> they could have it. I want to say these things that my
> position may be known to the people. My mode of life
> has been different from the life of some men.
> Circumstances that looked bad for me were misunder-
> stood. I have seen much of the world and I have always
> been taught to protect good women. My action in this
> matter was actuated by a desire to protect a good
> woman's name. Your honor, I am ready for sentence.

Bottom tried again to delay the judgment, but Judge
Butler brushed him aside. "These things have all been
threshed out time and again. There has been nothing new
brought out in this motion and sentence will be passed upon
the defendant." With that decision, Judge Butler pronounced
his verdict:

> The sentence of the court is that you be remanded to
> the custody of the commissioner of safety and ex-officio
> sheriff of the City and County of Denver; that within
> twenty-four hours you be taken by him, and delivered
> into the custody of the warden of the state penitentiary
> at Cañon City; that you be by the said warden kept in
> solitary confinement in the penitentiary until the
> week beginning Monday, October 27, 1913, ending
> Saturday, November 1, 1913; and that upon a day and
> hour in said week—to be designated by the warden—
> you be taken from said place of confinement to [a] place

of execution within the confines of said penitentiary, and then and there be hanged by the neck until you shall be dead.

There was a ray of hope. Judge Butler continued, "The court has no discretion in fixing the penalty for murder in the first degree. That is a matter solely for the jury.... I believe that the death penalty should be inflicted only in the most extreme cases. The facts here, in my opinion, take this case out of that class, and I therefore recommend that the governor commute this sentence to imprisonment at hard labor for life."

Back at the jailhouse, Henwood said he would refuse a commutation of his sentence from the governor, if one were granted. "What is death that I should fear it? Death has no suffering that I haven't now endured. But death linked with dishonor—to know that you must die with all of the filth, the rottenness with which this case has been surrounded, to serve you for a shroud—it is unthinkable, and yet it is better to die even so, with your face toward the front and fighting to give your innate decency a chance, than it is to accept a commutation of your sentence, which would amount to an admission of what the people said of you was true."

Turning to warden Kenney, Henwood asked, "John, you're not going to put me back in that death cell, are you? Surely you won't do that, will you?" Kenney promised he wouldn't. Henwood refused to discuss the case with gathered reporters, other than to say, "As long as there is life there is hope. There's no use of my trying my case in the newspapers again, by the press and in court. My case has been stated. I can say only I still have hope, and I am not afraid."

On December 23, Bottom asked the state Supreme Court for the second time to grant Henwood a new trial, based again on the contention that because the charge of murdering von Phul had been dismissed between the first and second trials, the Copeland charge also should have been dismissed. For good measure, he added that Rush's prejudicial misconduct in "bulldozing" witnesses and in his conduct toward Henwood created "reversible error."

The court took up the case on April 13, 1914, and handed down its denial of a new trial on July 8, virtually ending Henwood's hopes for freedom. It fixed Henwood's execution sometime during the week of October 25. In its decision, the court turned down Henwood's claim that when the charge of murdering von Phul was dismissed, the charge of killing Copeland should also be dismissed because the shootings constituted one act. Not so, said the court. Copeland's death was ruled a separate crime.

It was Kenney, who had grown close to Henwood during his time behind bars, who broke the news to him in the warden's office. "Frank, old man. I've bad news for you. They denied the appeal." Henwood stood silently and stared into space. He turned back to Kenney and said, "Well, I guess they want my death, and I suppose they'll get it. I'm sorry though. I had hoped that they would give me a chance to vindicate myself. The truth will be known sometime. I shall be vindicated, and it will be shown that I fired in self-defense. I hope it will be before I'm gone. I'd like to know that all men know I am an innocent man."

❖❖

Senator McCue's death in August 1913 sent Henwood further into depression. McCue and, after his death, his widow inexplicably championed Henwood's cause with financial and moral support almost from the day he was arrested following the shooting. McCue's widow remembered that her late husband told her, "What is friendship worth that cannot be tested by adversity?" She told friends that "Frank's unfailing courtesy, his strict sense of honor, his truthfulness, his enthusiasm over the deal he was preparing to put through made a deep and permanent impression on Mr. McCue. I believe with all my heart that Frank Henwood has been persecuted."

There were serious questions about Henwood's mental status when he suddenly attacked prisoner Francis E. Searway as the latter sat alone, eating. Henwood threw Searway to the floor and grabbed him by the throat, refusing to turn loose even though Searway's face turned blue and he lapsed into unconsciousness. It took three guards to pull Henwood away and return him to his cell. Henwood told the guards that other prisoners were making faces at him and that they smoked his pipe when he wasn't looking. He repeatedly told the warden that someone had placed "dictagraphs" in his cell. Some prisoners offered the opinion he was feigning insanity to stave off the state carrying out its death sentence, but his paranoia was clearly gaining control of him. His cellmate, Julius Hagan, a young Dane serving time for mail fraud, observed:

> I can't understand his actions at all. He used to be quite friendly, but he is the reverse now. From what little he says I have learned that he thinks I and the rest of us prisoners in this part of the jail are down on him. I don't believe he speaks twelve words a day to us. And another thing. He will start to talk about a subject and when he has gotten started he suddenly will stop in the middle of a sentence and walk away. He doesn't read his books or newspapers. He has almost given up eating, and when he eats, he eats the ordinary jail grub instead of the meals prepared for him at his expense by the jail cook. He spends practically all his time on his back. He lies there with his eyes wide open, looking at the ceiling, and never speaks a word.

Even more worrisome, Henwood hinted to Hagan, "There will be a change soon. Then you will think better of me." Hagan was puzzled. "I have never found out what he meant by that."

Raised Catholic, Henwood renewed his faith during his 1913 trial. Father Dominic Pantanello of Sacred Heart College (now Regis University) visited daily for religious instruction, and the two kneeled in prayer in Henwood's cell. Evangelist Jim Goodheart of the Sunshine Mission on Larimer Street, whose slogan was "A Hope for the Hopeless/A Friend to the Friendless," dropped in frequently to counsel the prisoner. The night before the jury returned its verdict in his second trial, Henwood kneeled beside his cot to pray. Exhausted by the three-week courtroom ordeal, he fell asleep with his head resting on the cot until guards came and lifted him into bed.

Though things looked bleak, Henwood continued to assure those around him that he felt confident, that he expected "to be a free man before the week is out. If I am acquitted by the jury as I expect to be, I shall immediately prepare for a trip into the heart of Alaska. And while I am away I shall tell the world my story from my own pen and in my own words just as it really was." Naturally, his account would portray himself as an unfortunate hero who came to the aid of a woman friend. His rival, Tony von Phul, was to be the bully.

Henwood's notoriety and good looks transformed him into a matinee idol during his incarceration. His confident demeanor, impeccable dress, and sensuous features made him the center of attention almost daily for the curious who crowded the lawn outside the West Side Court. To reporter Gene Fowler, "He had the aplomb of a dancing master and the eloquence of a minor poet." Accompanied by guards and his lawyers, he strode confidently between the jail to the courthouse, a slightly lopsided smirk on his face making him appear more confident than he was about the outcome of his trials. In his first trial, he wore a straw hat at a rakish angle, a hat he traded for an equally stylish derby in 1913.

Women found him alluring. During his second trial, two women seated in the courtroom gallery compared notes on him.

"I'd just like to go up and hug him," said one.

Her friend responded, as she knitted, "Who? Henwood?"

"Yes, I just think he's too lovely for anything."

"Ain't he? Have you ever seen them eyes?"

"Yes, and aren't they the dearest, most appealing things? Goodness! If I was on a jury I'd turn him loose in a minute."

The bailiff warned them to quiet down.

When he first entered the jail, Henwood was a likable prisoner. Everybody said so, and they appreciated that he shared the plentiful gifts—food, reading material, and clothing—that arrived daily from supporters. Fowler, who covered Henwood's 1911 trial and later became a notable author and screenwriter, recalled the dapper Henwood in the 1946 book, *Denver Murders*,

> Henwood was a somewhat serious-minded fellow, as who wouldn't be when being condemned to life imprisonment in the pen? I don't think he had any sense of humor even before he shot von Phul. But he was a whimsical fellow, tall, bald, with rather loose lips but nice eyes. His forehead was high, quite aside from the fact that he was bald, but the baldness accentuated his height. He walked a little stooped. I should say he weighed 192 pounds and was easily six feet tall. He wore well-tailored clothes and was always well-shaven, and indeed looked like an intellectual warden rather than a prisoner.

❖

On October 16, less than two weeks before his scheduled execution, Henwood received the commutation he said he would turn down. Governor Elias M. Ammons signed an executive order giving Henwood life in prison instead of hanging.

"The policy of capital punishment is not involved," Ammons wrote. "The only question to be determined [is] whether the death penalty in this case is excessive." Ammons was answering the recommendation of Judge Butler and also the pleadings of John Springer, who appeared before the parole board and told his story of the circumstances surrounding the affair between his wife and von Phul. "I would have killed von Phul myself had I known the situation; this man Henwood butted into my business." He explained the results of his own investigation into von Phul's behavior with Isabel Springer before the shooting,

> I have spent thousands trying to learn the truth of this matter, and it has not been in vain. Isabel's mother on her deathbed sent word to me that von Phul had threatened in her presence to kill Isabel with a revolver which he pointed at her. Von Phul was holding over my wife's head letters she had written years before. He blackmailed her and was trying to get diamonds and money from her. Instead of coming to me, she went to my friend, Henwood, a man I had helped and placed where he could earn a living.

Rush called the commutation "a travesty. The action of the board of pardons is but in line with its past record of helping murderers escape the penalties imposed by verdicts of juries and judgments of courts. It is poor encouragement to those of us who are trying to make murder unpopular in this city." For Springer's story of blackmail, Rush had one word: "Piffle!"

"God bless the governor," Henwood exulted. "I have lived in hell for fifteen months, the hell of doubt, the hell of uncertainty, the hell of waiting, waiting. But today I can see the light even in my cell and I know I live. Good God, it has been awful! I have learned that I love life. I am a nervous wreck. I am a shadow, a walking phantom, yet with my few remaining faculties of thought and desire I cling to the body, to the life, to the living. I have been mad at times and in my lucid moments I have oftentimes questioned whether or not I was wholly mad all the time."

The next day, a rejuvenated Henwood rose early and wrote letters to friends and family. He carefully arranged his personal effects, including a scarf pin, a book, a cigarette case, a pocket-knife, a watch and chain, and a ring, on a table. "I want those who have been my friends to have something of mine that may testify mutely after I have gone up there [Cañon City]. To whom are they being given? That I will not tell. They are going to be given to my friends, and none but the recipients shall know." On October 18, he was transported by train to the penitentiary in Cañon City to spend the rest of his life.

Accompanied by deputy sheriffs William Arnett, Robert Thompson, and Samuel Pollard, and another prisoner, Dave Minton, who was serving eighteen months for larceny, Henwood left the County Jail at 7 A.M. and walked to Union Depot by way of Speer Boulevard, Market Street, and Seventeenth Street, his first time away from the jail since the cell door clanged shut behind him in the wee hours of May 25, 1911. Except for a group of firemen at City Hall and two dozen people at the depot, his 8 A.M. departure aboard the Denver & Rio Grande's Pacific Coast Limited went almost unnoticed. Only two friends—Bottom, his attorney, and Mrs. Thomas McCue, the widow of his financial benefactor—were there to see him off.

An estimated three hundred onlookers were waiting at the Cañon City depot and lining the streets to the prison when the train arrived after a five-and-a-half-hour journey from Denver, 160 miles to the north. It was a much-changed man who stepped off the train. His clothes hung loosely on his lank frame, and his face was a pasty pallor. His mood was upbeat, and he chatted lightly with his guards, but his face darkened when the stone walls of the prison and a crowd milling around the front gates came into view. Those waiting were denied a look at him. He was taken in a side entrance

A haggard Frank Henwood photographed at the state penitentiary on October 18, 1914. (Courtesy of the Colorado State Archives)

at 1:40 P.M. Inside the walls, his mood improved. He took a deep breath and told a guard, "It's much better here than at the County Jail, and I know I am going to be satisfied."

Like any other inmate, Henwood, now thirty-seven, was issued white-and-black striped prison garb, given a shave and photographed, front and side, and traded his name for a number. Until his death, he would be number 9318. When he was admitted to the prison on October 18, 1914, he was listed as standing 5-foot-11 and weighing 147 pounds. In addition to various scars, he had two vaccination marks on his left arm. The admission report noted, "Teeth good—four gold, two upper left, one lower left and one lower right." Most revealing, under the category "Temperate" were written the words "No—Morphine." He and Mrs. Springer shared more than their love of theater and societal gatherings.

Henwood fit into prison life quickly. He was assigned to

the carpentry shop, a job, it turned out, for which he had considerable skill. He was a model prisoner. Unfortunately, his time behind bars had left him fragile mentally. Despite the governor's commutation, Henwood believed he was going to be hanged. Every Friday, known to the prisoners as "death day" because it was the day hangings took place, Henwood became incapacitated, unable to work, and waited by his cell door for the warden to take him on that last long walk. No amount of persuasion by prison officials could change his mind. Some feared he was becoming insane, consumed with paranoia. He believed that unnamed persons were putting "odious thoughts" into his head and trying to induce him to confess as he slept.

His mental state worsened in 1916 when his wife, whom he had not seen in years, filed for divorce because he was a felon. In 1917 came the news of the death in New York City to drugs and alcohol of Isabel Patterson Springer, the woman for whom he had risked his life.

He was fighting an uphill battle, mentally and physically. In April 1921, he was among twenty-one murderers who sought pardons for their crimes. He was turned down, for the second time.

❖

A year later, Governor Oliver Shoup issued an executive order granting Henwood clemency, with the stipulation that he never return to Denver. The governor acted after prodding by John Springer, who broke into tears in his appeal before the governor, by the ever-faithful Mrs. McCue, and by a group of influential, and wealthy, supporters.

An angry Judge Butler wrote to Shoup. "Life is altogether too cheap in Colorado. The small value it now possesses ought not to be still further reduced." He reminded Shoup that when he and former state Supreme Court Chief Justice W. H. Gabbert recommended that Henwood's sentence be commuted from death to life imprisonment, "we meant for life and not one day less." Henwood, Judge Butler told Shoup, "should be let out only when dead. Two juries found him guilty of murder, and two judges sentenced him. It appears that friends can organize and by persistent effort can eventually procure his pardon."

Tony von Phul's cousin, Henry, the former Cripple Creek sheriff, was even more to the point. The day Henwood walked out of prison, von Phul wrote to the governor, "You have seen fit to release from the penitentiary Harold F. Henwood, a degenerate lounge lizard and make-believe society man and double murderer. You should be ashamed of yourself for degrading the high office you now occupy. You might try paroling him to St. Louis or Cripple Creek, where his friends would be especially interested in his welfare."

Nevertheless, Henwood, wearing a steel gray suit and a straw hat and carrying a new suitcase, walked out of the penitentiary gate at 4:20 P.M. on May 28, 1922. In his pants pocket was a five-dollar bill, a going-away gift from the state. John Bottom and Mrs. McCue were there to greet him.

Four days after his release, Henwood had an accidental encounter with a *Denver Post* reporter on a train and vowed he was ready to make a new start. "I am going to work hard to prove that I am not the worthless pup many people believe me to be. I am going to make good. Never again am I going to touch liquor. I am going to tend strictly to my own business. Butting in on other people's business got me into all my trouble."

With help from Mrs. McCue, Henwood moved to New Mexico and began a new life under the name Francis Collins and appeared to be getting his life straightened out. He became assistant manager of a hotel in Socorro, New Mexico, with promises from the hotel's owner that he would be made a partner in the enterprise. But Henwood's instability, which had dogged him since his privileged youth, his time as a world traveler, and his brief episode in Denver, got the best of him again.

Only ten months after his release, he was returned to a cell in Cañon City after he threatened to kill a young woman because she refused to marry him. It constituted a violation of his release, and he was back behind bars, this time for good, on March 26, 1923. Henwood continued to enlist support from friends and lawyers for his release but it was not to be. His health deteriorated, and his weight fell alarmingly. In hopes that removing his tonsils would improve his condition, he was operated on by Cañon City physician Dr. E. C. Webb on September 27, 1929. At 6:45 A.M. the next day, with only a nurse attending him, Henwood died of "acute dilation of the heart." He was fifty-two.

He had a premonition of his demise. Four days before he died, he wrote a letter to Boulder attorney Michael Rinn, whose appeal to Governor Billy Adams for commutation because of Henwood's failing health had been denied. Henwood pleaded to Rinn:

> The truth is, dear Mike, I am dying on my feet. I have just one fighting chance to live. That is to get out and get to Hot Springs, Arkansas. God knows that each day takes just a little more of what strength I've got left, and with my weight around 117 pounds, instead of 187, which I formerly weighed, it's pretty hard digging. No one here or in Denver realizes all that the loss of a single day means to me in my fast-weakening condition.

At the request of his mother in her will, Frank Henwood, who never found a permanent home while he was alive, was laid to rest forever beside his parents, Harold and Margaret, in Holy Name Cemetery in Jersey City, New Jersey.

He spent fourteen years, eleven months, and ten days in the Cañon City penitentiary "because I did just what any other man would have done under the circumstances." He swore to the end that he acted only to save his friend's marriage and to protect Isabel Springer.

As his life neared its end, he grew reflective. He told a reporter for the *Rocky Mountain News*: "There's a moral to my case, that every young man ought to have a vocation. It saves regret, it saves remorse. It paves the way to clean living. I think that I suffered from having too much money. I tried hard enough to make good but every career requires a certain amount of education along practical lines. It was that which I had just commenced to acquire when this thing happened.

"I have regrets."

The Henwood family memorial, Holy Name Cemetery, Jersey City, New Jersey. (Dick Kreck collection)

Epilogue

Isabel Patterson Springer's headstone, Fair View Cemetery, Fairview, New Jersey. (Dick Kreck collection)

IN THE COURSE of researching this book, I discovered that Isabel Patterson Springer slept forever beneath the grass of the Fair View Cemetery in New Jersey without a headstone.

Fulcrum publisher Robert Baron and I agreed that this was an ignoble end for the beguiling Mrs. Springer, so we split the cost of having a simple granite headstone placed on her grave in the summer of 2002. It reads, "Isabel Patterson Springer/ "Sassy"/1880–1917." Long after her death, the cautionary tale of Isabel's rise and fall as one of the most beautiful and admired women of her time in Denver still draws men to her.

I'm glad she no longer lies in an unmarked grave.

John Springer's Cross Country Ranch went through a long metamorphosis after Springer's daughter Annie became the owner. Annie and her husband, Lafayette Hughes, sold the ranch to Oklahoma oilman Waite Phillips, who renamed it Sunland Ranch, then sold it and the adjoining Wolhurst estate to Frank Kistler in 1926. Kistler renamed the ranch Diamond K, but when he was left bankrupt by the stock-market crash of 1929, he sold it for $375,000 to Lawrence Phipps Jr., who called it Highland Ranch. Marvin Davis owned it briefly before selling it to the Mission Viejo Company, which planned a subdivision that became home to ninety thousand residents. The Highlands Ranch suburb south of Denver is now the largest town in Douglas County.

The original Springer castle on the ranch property, much modified and enlarged from its earliest days, stands empty in its magnificence and is used occasionally today for charity events.

John Springer sold his seven-bedroom mansion at 930 Washington Street to Frank R. Read for thirty thousand dollars in 1910, and in 1926 it was sold to the family of Irene Frye Gay. In 2002, Mrs. Gay still owned the house, operated as the Frye Apartments.

The Brown Palace lives on in its splendor, still a center of social activity. Ellyngton's restaurant satisfies today's guests in the space once occupied by the hotel's dining room. The Marble Bar, where Frank Henwood and Tony von Phul met in a murderous confrontation, still serves as a bar, Churchill's, that provides a masculine environment with cigars and hard liquor much in evidence. The Brown Palace Hotel, still Denver's finest, remains to this day the place for classy affairs.

—Dick Kreck

Murder at the Brown Palace: A Chronology

1907

April 27: Isabel Patterson Folck and John W. Springer marry in St. Louis.

1910

November 2: Frank Henwood arrives in Denver.

1911

May 23: Tony von Phul arrives in Denver.

May 24: Henwood shoots, mortally wounds von Phul and George Copeland and seriously wounds James W. Atkinson at the Brown Palace Hotel.

May 25: Von Phul dies at St. Luke's Hospital at 11:20 A.M.

June 1: Copeland dies at St. Luke's at 12:20 A.M. Henwood pleads not guilty to charge of killing von Phul.

June 2: Henwood pleads not guilty to charge of killing Copeland. Trial in Copeland case set for June 18.

June 10: Application for continuance denied.

June 20: First trial commences.

June 28: Trial ends. Jury retires at 10:30 P.M.

June 29: Jury returns verdict of guilty of murder in the second degree.

July 1: Springer granted a divorce from Isabel Patterson Springer.

July 28: Henwood's motion for a new trial denied by District Judge Greeley Whitford. Henwood sentenced to life in prison.

September 27: Application for a delay in carrying out the verdict filed with the state Supreme Court.

1913

February 3: Henwood granted a new trial on charge of killing Copeland; by the state Supreme Court freed of count of murdering von Phul.

March 24: Plea of former acquittal in Copeland case not allowed.

May 28: Second trial on charge of murdering Copeland begins.

June 18: Jury returns verdict of guilty in the first degree, fixes the penalty at death.

June 28: Verdict appealed to Judge Charles C. Butler.

July 18: Appeal denied by Judge Butler.

July 27: Henwood sentenced to be hanged the week of October 27. Judge Butler asks Governor Elias M. Ammons to commute the penalty to life in prison.

September 15: Henwood granted a sixty-day stay by state Supreme Court.

December 23: Case appealed to state Supreme Court for a second time.

1914

April 13: Appeal heard by Supreme Court.

July 8: Supreme Court affirms decision of lower court. Hanging set for week of October 25.

October 4: Supreme Court denies petition for rehearing.

October 16: Governor Ammons commutes Henwood's sentence to life in prison.

October 18: Henwood transported by train from Denver to the state penitentiary in Cañon City, Colorado.

1917

April 19: Isabel Patterson Springer dies at Blackwell's Island, New York City, at the age of thirty-seven.

October 23: Henwood asks for pardon.

1918

December 14: Henwood denied mitigation of original sentence by state pardons board.

1921

April 18: Henwood makes second appeal for pardon.

November 17: Pardon denied again.

1922

May 26: Henwood granted executive clemency by Governor Oliver Shoup and moves to New Mexico.

1923

March 26: Henwood is returned to the state penitentiary for parole violation.

1929

September 28: Frank Henwood dies at the state penitentiary, Cañon City, at the age of fifty-two.

1945

January 10: John W. Springer, age eighty-five, dies in Littleton, Colorado.

Notes on Sources

Chapter One
Prelude to Murder

As they did throughout the time of the murders and trials, Denver's four fiercely competitive newspapers (*The Denver Post*, the *Rocky Mountain News*, *The Denver Times*, and *The Denver Republican*) printed story after story, most of them factual. They were an invaluable source, mainly for the courtroom testimony, because the original documents have disappeared from the Colorado State Archives. The folders remain but the paperwork is gone, pilfered by persons unknown.

The bulk of the conversations between Frank Henwood and Tony von Phul comes from courtroom testimony by Henwood and, to a much lesser extent, others. A good account of the murders and the events that led up to them are in *Timber Line*, Gene Fowler's entertaining though often embellished history of *The Post* and its two founders, Frederick Bonfils and Harry Tammen. The murder is given passing retelling in various histories of the Brown Palace Hotel, although the background of the participants is generally glossed over.

Chapter Two
The Shooting

A point of constant disagreement between prosecutors and Henwood's defense team was whether Tony von Phul turned his back on Henwood after knocking him down in the bar of the Brown Palace. Prosecuting attorneys frequently referred to a wound in von Phul's back, while Henwood's lawyers maintained that von Phul fixed Henwood with a hateful stare. Most witnesses agreed that von Phul had turned away from Henwood after decking him with one punch.

Newspaper reporters, court officials, and other observers rarely agreed on Frank Henwood's name. His given name was Harold Francis Henwood, but he was called Frank H. Henwood, Harold F. Henwood, Harold Henwood (his father's name), F. H. Henwood, H. F. Henwood, and other variations.

A reasonably accurate account of the shooting is contained in the chapter called "Murder at the Brown Palace," part of a compilation of stories on peculiar crimes that appeared in the 1946 book *Denver Murders*, edited by Lee Casey.

The appearance of *Follies of 1910* at the Broadway Theater in May 1911 was a highlight of that year's theater season. Flo Ziegfeld, his shows, and his career are related in an excellent history, *The Ziegfeld Touch*, by Richard and Paulette Ziegfeld.

CHAPTER THREE

Tony von Phul

Sylvester Louis "Tony" von Phul was a legend in St. Louis, his hometown. His balloon adventures and his way with beautiful women raised him to matinee-idol status. His exploits in various ballooning competitions were covered frequently by the St. Louis press.

Some newspaper accounts claimed that von Phul and Isabel Patterson Springer were high school classmates in St. Louis and, maybe, childhood sweethearts. No evidence could be found to corroborate what were little more than rumors. Much of the biographical information on von Phul came from a generally glowing account of his life in the *St. Louis Republic* of May 23, 1909. His balloon-riding exploits are mentioned at some length in reminiscences by his friend

Maj. Albert Bond Lambert in the June 1928 issue of the *Missouri Historical Society Magazine.*

CHAPTER FOUR

Frank Henwood

Reporters for Denver's newspapers were given extraordinary access to Henwood and his jail cell. A glib and social promoter, Henwood became friends with many of those who covered him.

It can be a confusing matter to understand whether Henwood was tried for killing von Phul or his other victim, George Copeland. Prosecutors decided they stood a better chance of getting a conviction over Copeland's death, but most of the testimony was about Henwood's fear of von Phul and about whether Henwood acted in self-defense. Henwood was never on trial for killing von Phul, only for the accidental death of Copeland, a barroom bystander.

Exception and *incompetency* are legal terms dealing with courtroom procedure. An exception is a lawyer's way of establishing in the record that he disagrees with a court's ruling and gives the court an opportunity to change its mind. It also lays the basis for an appeal. (It is no longer required in Colorado courts.) Incompetency refers to evidence so lacking in credibility that it is not admissible.

That Isabel Springer's adventures with her two lovers were probably well known around town prior to the shooting may be inferred from the fact that only two days passed before her name appeared in newspapers, suggesting her as a cause of the friction between the two principals.

The 1906 murder case of Harry K. Thaw, Evelyn Nesbit, and Stanford White, remarkably similar to the Denver shooting and scandal, is covered in a February 1999 *Smithsonian Magazine* article, "Pictures of a Tragedy," and in detail in *The Architect of Desire*, by Suzannah Lessard. The story is also one of the key subplots in E. L. Doctorow's best-selling novel *Ragtime* (later made into a Hollywood film).

Chapter Five
John Springer
The life of John Wallace Springer is chronicled in Wilbur Fiske Stone's *History of Colorado*.

Polly Pry frequently criticized Springer and his political ambitions in a magazine that bore her name. She was best known as *The Denver Post's* "sob sister," a teller of sad tales.

The incredibly crooked mayoral campaign of 1904, in which Robert W. Speer defeated John Springer, is dealt with in reformer George Creel's *Rebel at Large*. Political corruption in general is detailed by David Graham Phillips in *The Muckrakers*, edited by Arthur and Lila Weinberg.

Former Denver Mayor Quigg Newton, whose mother was John Springer's niece, was particularly helpful in providing access to a scrapbook containing newspaper clippings and other memorabilia chronicling Springer's political career.

Chapter Six
Guilty
The Denver Post, The Denver Times, and the *Rocky Mountain News* ran more or less complete transcriptions of Frank Henwood's testimony in their June 23, 1911, editions.

Henwood's excoriation of Judge Greeley Whitford after he was found guilty of second-degree murder may be unequaled in American judicial history. It was within Whitford's authority to give Henwood a sentence of as little as ten years—but after Henwood's lecture, Whitford sentenced him to life in prison. Henwood's entire diatribe appeared in *The Post* on July 28, 1911.

Chapter Seven
Isabel Springer
Men's fascination with Isabel Springer is rather difficult to unravel at this late date. She was a beautiful creature, and

accounts of her personality described her as vivacious and high-spirited, but she was a high-maintenance attachment. She was a poor judge of her admirers. Like many women of her time, she was beginning to find interests outside the home, a phenomenon chronicled in Henry Allen's *What It Felt Like.*

The city's society writers fawned over Isabel and her theatrical interests, describing her in glowing terms when she first arrived as John Springer's constant companion in the summer of 1906. Their praise quickly turned to disapproval when her role in the scandal become public in 1911.

Isabel's trail grew vague after her departure from Denver. It is clear that her addiction to drugs and alcohol was severe. She managed in the years between 1911 and her death to spend all of the rather generous settlement she received from her cuckolded husband.

Her friendship with Audrey Munson, the premier nude model of her generation, was an odd one. Though Munson was a top-flight model and noted silent-film actress (one of the first to disrobe for the motion-picture camera), Isabel was merely a bit player. Munson wrote, in an often-melodramatic newspaper series called "Queen of the Artists' Studios," how drugs and alcohol took a toll on Isabel's legendary beauty.

CHAPTER EIGHT
The Reason

The only known accounts of Isabel Springer's series of impassioned letters to Tony von Phul were carried by *The Denver Post* and *The Denver Republican*, mainly in 1913. The newspapers only hint at whether the "unprintable" ones were more graphic. The published letters were relatively tame by current standards, little more than mash notes.

John Springer managed to have Isabel's letters expunged from their divorce case and, though several copies of them were made, none has surfaced since some of them were printed in the Denver papers.

CHAPTER NINE
A Second Chance
Denver Post reporter Frances "Pinky" Wayne, so named for the color of her hair, spent a great deal of time with Henwood after his arrest. Her reports, such as the one in which she described his appearance as "ghastly," have a strong sense of disapproval about them.

The shrill squabbling between opposing attorneys can scarcely be imagined today. The give-and-take between John Bottom and prosecutor John Rush, particularly hostile, was printed word-for-word in *The Post* of March 10, 1913. The West Side Court, scene of many high-profile trials, was often a legal battleground but rarely at this level of animosity.

The Post's antigun, antiviolence stance was surprisingly modern for its time.

CHAPTER TEN
An Old Friend
John Springer's appearance on the witness stand took everyone by surprise. His refusal to testify in the 1911 trial was never explained, although embarrassment and his divorce were probably leading causes. His appearance in 1913 came after much soul-searching until he was clear in his mind that Henwood was acting on his behalf in the matter. His testimony and his courtroom encounter with Henwood are detailed in *The Denver Post* of June 17, 1913.

CHAPTER ELEVEN
The Final Verdict
Henwood was a broken man after his second conviction. It was about this time that his mental state began to become a concern among his friends and jail keepers. His erratic behavior and outbursts of anger became more frequent. A good account of his state appeared in the June 19, 1913,

edition of the *Rocky Mountain News*.

Author Gene Fowler, who covered the Henwood trials as a young reporter for *The Post*, found Henwood an engaging fellow and recounted his remembrances of him in *Denver Murders*.

Although it is a legal fine point, there is a difference between Henwood being released on "executive privilege" by Governor Oliver Shoup and receiving a parole. Executive privilege is at the discretion of the governor while a parole is a statutory option. The effect was the same: Henwood was released from prison, and newspapers and others spoke of him being given a "parole."

Bibliography

Articles

"A Portfolio of Early Aviation Pictures." *Bulletin of the Missouri Historical Society*, volume III, no. 4, July 1952.

Davidson, Levette J. "The Festival of Mountain and Plain." *The Colorado Magazine*, Colorado Historical Society, July 1948.

———. "The Festival of Mountain and Plain." *The Colorado Magazine*, Colorado Historical Society, September 1948.

DeLorme, Roland L. "Turn-of-the-Century Denver: An Invitation to Reform." *The Colorado Magazine*, XLV/I, Colorado Historical Society, 1968.

Horgan, James. "City of Flight: The History of Aviation in St. Louis." *Missouri Historical Society Magazine*, April 1965.

Kelly, Bernard. "No Place Like 'The Brown'." *Empire* magazine, *The Denver Post*, January 21, 1968.

Lambert, Major Albert Bond. "Early History of Aeronautics in St. Louis." *Missouri Historical Society Magazine*, June 1928.

Melrose, Frances. "Denver's Classic Society Crime." *Rocky Mountain News*, March 10, 1946.

———. "A Beautiful Woman." *Rocky Mountain News*, April 5, 1992.

————. "When Denver Society Was Rocked by Illicit Love and Murder." *Rocky Mountain News*, April 30, 1995.

Mitchell, J. Paul. "Municipal Reform in Denver: The Defeat of Mayor Speer." *The Colorado Magazine*, XLV/I, CHS, 1968.

Park, Edwards. "Pictures of a Tragedy." *Smithsonian Magazine*, February 1999.

Pry, Polly. *Polly Pry: A Journal of Comment and Criticism*, September 10, 17, and 24, 1904.

Springer, John W. "The American Coach Horse—The Automobile's Effect Upon the Horse." *The Horse Show Monthly*, n.d. Copy in author's possession.

————. Eulogy at the Bier of Colonel William Frederick Cody, Denver, January 14, 1917. Microfilm roll 3, Buffalo Bill scrapbooks, 1887–1891, Buffalo Bill Museum, Cody, Wyoming.

Whearley, Robert. "They Tried to Keep Lively Mrs. Springer Out of It." *Rocky Mountain News*, November 9, 1954.

BOOKS

Allen, Henry. *What It Felt Like: Living in the American Century*. New York: Pantheon, 1999.

Brinkley, Douglas. *History of the United States*. New York: Viking, 1998.

Caffrey, Kate. *The 1900s Lady*. London: Gordon & Cremonesi, 1976.

Chiasson Jr., Lloyd. *The Press on Trial: Crimes and Trials as Media Events*. Westport, Conn.: Greenwood Press, 1997.

Cole, Henry G. *Confessions of an American Opium Eater*. Boston: J. H. Earle, 1895.

Creel, George. *Rebel at Large*. New York: Putnam, 1947.

Downing, Sybil, and Robert E. Smith. *Tom Patterson: Colorado Crusader for Change*. Niwot, Colo.: University Press of Colorado, 1995.

Ferril, William Columbus. *Sketches of Colorado*. Denver: Western Press Bureau Company, 1911.

Fowler, Gene. *Timber Line: A Story of Bonfils and Tammen*. New York: Garden City Books, 1933.

Gibson, Barbara. *The City Club of Denver 1922–1997*. Denver: City Club, 1999.

Goodstein, Phil. *The Ghosts of Denver: Capitol Hill*. Denver: New Social Publications, 1996.

Halliday, Brett. "Murder at the Brown Palace." In *Denver Murders*, edited by Lee Casey. New York: Duell, Sloan and Pearce, 1946.

Holliday, J. S. *The World Rushed In*. New York: Simon & Schuster, 1981.

Hosokawa, Bill. *Thunder in the Rockies: The Incredible Denver Post*. New York: Morrow, 1976.

Johnson, Charles A. *Denver's Mayor Speer*. Denver: Bighorn, 1969.

Kasson, Joy S. *Buffalo Bill's Wild West: Celebrity, Memory and Popular History*. New York: Hill and Wang, 2000.

Korn, Jerry, ed. *This Fabulous Century*, Vol. I, *1900–1910*. New York: Time-Life Books, 1969.

———. *This Fabulous Century*, Vol. II, *1910–1920*. New York: Time-Life Books, 1969.

Leonard, Stephen J., and Thomas J. Noel. *Denver: Mining Camp to Metropolis*. Niwot, Colo.: University Press of Colorado, 1990.

Lessard, Suzannah. *The Architect of Desire*. New York: Dell, 1996.

Lindsey, Ben B., and Harvey J. O'Higgins. *The Beast*. New York: Doubleday, 1910.

Mangen, Terry Wm. *Colorado on Glass*. Denver: Sundance, 1980.

Marquis Who Was Who in America, volume IV, 1961–68. Chicago: Who's Who Inc., 1968.

Marr, Josephine Lowell. *Douglas County: A Historical Journey*, compiled by Joan Marr Keiser. Gunnison, Colo.: B&B Printers, 1983.

Morgan, H. Wayne. *Yesterday's Addicts: American Society and Drug Abuse, 1865–1920*. Norman, Okla.: University of Oklahoma Press, 1973.

Noel, Thomas J. *The City and the Saloon: Denver, 1858–1916*. Niwot, Colorado: University Press of Colorado, 1996.

Parkhill, Forbes. *The Wildest of the West*. Denver: Sage Books, 1953.

Perkin, Robert L. *The First Hundred Years*. Garden City, N.J.: Doubleday, 1959.

Rozas, Diane, and Anita Bourne Gottehrer. *American Venus: The Extraordinary Life of Audrey Munson, Model and Muse*. Los Angeles: Balcony Press, 1999.

Ronzio, Richard A. *Silver Images of Colorado*. Denver: Sundance, 1986.

Sinclair, Upton. *The Brass Check*. Pasadena, Calif.: Upton Sinclair, 1920.

Smiley, Jerome C. *History of Denver*. Denver: Times-Sun, 1901.

Sprague, Marshall. *Colorado: A Bicentennial History*. New York: Norton, 1976.

Stone, Wilbur Fiske. *History of Colorado*, Deluxe Supplement. Chicago: Clarke, 1918).

———. *History of Colorado*, Volume V. Chicago: Clarke, 1919.

Thode, Jackson. *George L. Beam and the Denver & Rio Grande*. Vol. 1. Denver: Sundance, 1987.

Van Cise, Philip S. *Fighting the Underworld*. New York: Houghton Mifflin, 1936.

Weinberg, Arthur, and Lila, eds. *The Muckrakers*. New York: Simon and Schuster, 1961.

Whiteside, Henry O. *Menace in the West: Colorado and the American Experience with Drugs, 1873–1963*. Denver: Colorado Historical Society, 1997.

Ziegfeld, Richard, and Paulette. *The Ziegfeld Touch: The Life and Times of Florenz Ziegfeld Jr.* New York: Harry N. Abrams, 1993.

ADDITIONAL SOURCES FOR HISTORICAL REFERENCE

LIBRARIES AND MUSEUMS

Buffalo Bill Museum: Cody, Wyoming

Cañon City Historical Society: Cañon City, Colorado

Chicago Public Library

Colorado Historical Society: Denver

Colorado State Archives: Denver

The Denver Post library

Douglas Public Library: Castle Rock, Colorado

Huntington Library: Pasadena, California

Library of Congress: Washington, D.C.

Littleton Historical Society: Littleton, Colorado

Missouri Historical Society: St. Louis, Missouri

Newberry Library: Chicago

Shubert Archive: New York City

Roy O. West Library, DePauw University: Greencastle, Indiana

Western History and Genealogy Department, Denver Public Library

MANUSCRIPTS

Cleveland, Lenna May, Cleveland Family Collection, Colorado State Historical Society, 1982.

Kuykendall, Cora Eddelman, "Roots and Memories," Local History Collection, Douglas Public Library, Castle Rock, Colorado, 1986.

NEWSPAPERS

Arapahoe Herald, Littleton, Colorado

Colorado Springs Gazette

Chicago Daily Tribune

Daily Record, Cañon City, Colorado

Denver Express

The Denver Newsletter and Colorado Advertiser

The Denver Post

The Denver Republican

The Denver Times

Hot Springs Sentinel-Record, Arkansas

Leadville Courier, Colorado

The New York Times

Ouray Plain Dealer, Colorado

Rocky Mountain Herald, Denver

Rocky Mountain News, Denver

Socorro Chieftain, New Mexico

St. Louis Globe-Democrat

St. Louis Post-Dispatch

St. Louis Republic

St. Louis Star